THE WINTERTHUR GUIDE TO

Recognizing Styles

AMERICAN DECORATIVE ARTS FROM THE 17TH THROUGH 19TH CENTURIES

COMPILED BY PAULINE K. EVERSMANN

HENRY FRANCIS DU PONT WINTERTHUR MUSEUM
WINTERTHUR, DELAWARE

DISTRIBUTED BY UNIVERSITY PRESS OF NEW ENGLAND
HANOVER AND LONDON

SERIES EDITOR: *Onie Rollins*

CONTENT EDITOR: *Lisa L. Lock*

COPY EDITOR: *Teresa A. Vivolo*

DESIGNER: *Abby Goldstein*

෬

Manufactured in Singapore by C. S. Graphics

LIBRARY OF CONGRESS CATALOGING-IN-PUBLICATION DATA

Henry Francis du Pont Winterthur Museum.
    The Winterthur guide to recognizing styles : American decorative arts from the 17th through 19th centuries / compiled by Pauline K. Eversmann.
        p. cm.
Includes bibliographical references.
    ISBN 0-912724-51-x
    1. Decorative arts–United States–History. I. Eversmann, Pauline K., 1942-II. Title.

NK805 .H43   2001
745' .09–dc21

2001002664

TABLE OF CONTENTS

FIG. 1. Lady's cabinet and writing table

INTRODUCTION

Understanding Style

$\mathcal{T}$hink about how many different ways you use or hear people use the word *style*. We describe people as having style, talk about a person's lifestyle, or refer to musical compositions as being in a certain style. Entrees on a menu can be prepared in the style of a particular country or region, and most Sunday newspapers have a section titled "Style" that contains everything from articles on fashion to wedding announcements to descriptions of the latest design trends. None of these uses are incorrect. The word *style* can be applied to music, literary works, objects, events, or performances. *Style* can even be applied to the characteristic ways in which some people think or behave.

In the decorative and fine arts, the term *style* is used most often to describe a specific set of visual characteristics. Learning to identify visual characteristics is the first step in recognizing different styles. The ability to recognize a style requires a devotion to careful observation and to creating a set of mental images upon which to draw for reference. We see style when we notice visual characteristics—design elements—repeated over and over again in a group of objects. You cannot define a particular style by one object; it is the recognition of similar elements in many objects that leads to the identification of a style.

Recognizing styles is an ongoing exercise in comparisons and contrasts. It involves developing the habit of active looking. This method of active looking is referred to as *aesthetic analysis* by art historians. There are several important char-

acteristics to look for when analyzing an object in order to determine its stylistic category. These include line, proportion, volume, ornamentation, texture, material,
color, and scale. For the purposes of learning to recognize styles in decorative art
objects, the most important are line, ornamentation, and color. Proportion, volume,
and texture are also to be carefully considered. Two objects, a late eighteenth-
century lady's cabinet and writing table (fig. 1) and a seventeenth-century chest (fig.
2), serve as examples of these characteristics.

LINE describes borders, angles, and curves. Line also refers to the overall form or
outline of an object as well as the lines within an object. Both the writing table, or
desk, and the chest are composed of straight lines; they are box forms, defined by
straight lines meeting at right angles. Both also feature smaller rectangles contained
within a basic box form. Curved lines are confined primarily to ornamentation: the
turned spindles on the chest and the glass ovals in the cabinet.

PROPORTION describes how the various dimensions of an object and the size of
its various parts relate to one another. Both the chest and writing table are sym-
metrical, but their proportions are different. The chest is equally proportioned
throughout—each row of drawers is exactly the same height. The three distinct sec-
tions of the writing table (the lower dresser, the middle section with three oval panels, and the upper section with mirror) are deliberately "stepped" in both height
and depth to give the substantial case piece balance atop the tall, slender legs.

VOLUME describes the way an object takes up space. Volume can be defined not
only by how large an object is but also by whether it is framed compactly or
has extensions and by the relationship of solids and voids within it. The chest
appears to be massive compared to the writing table because of the way in which
the long, slender legs of the table and the void they outline visually lighten its substantial form.

ORNAMENTATION refers to the decorative elements of an object. Ornamentation
may be integral to the form of the object or it may be applied to the surface.
Ornament may sometimes be the most readily identifiable indicator of a particular
style. The applied, turned half-spindles and brightly painted abstract designs on the
chest are ornaments that can be identified as designs that were popular in the seventeenth century. The writing table's decorative motifs all speak to the federal era,
when a revived interest in classicism dictated fashion: the interplay of geometric

shapes and the use of such classical motifs as mythological figures in the glass insets and the dome-shape finials are clues to the fact that the lady's cabinet and writing table was made in the late eighteenth century.

TEXTURE indicates the relative roughness or smoothness of a material as it presents itself to our eyes or to our touch. The use of applied and carved ornamentation

FIG. 2. Seventeenth-century chest

on the chest gives it a deeply textured surface, whereas the veneer and glass panels on the writing table are laid flush to preserve an essentially smooth, flat surface.

MATERIAL is the substance that composes an object or its parts. Material dictates the relative ease or difficulty in manipulating line, color, ornamentation, and texture. The chest is built from solid oak; decoration was applied to the surface, and ornament was carved into the wood. The writing table, however, is made from multiple materials: mahogany inlaid with strips of satinwood, glass insets, and brass hardware.

COLOR describes the hue, value, and saturation of the shades we see. While we are familiar with such concepts as bright red and dark red, we often do not think of color in terms of these characteristics. The *hues* are the names we have assigned to colors. *Value* implies the amount of white or black that an artist mixes with pigments to achieve ranges such as "bright red" or "dark red." *Saturation* suggests how vivid or intense the color is. There is high contrast in the chest between the black-painted spindles and the vivid hues used to decorate the drawer fronts. The writing table contains contrasting tonal values in the light veneers and dark inlays as well as from the bright gold used to highlight the domes and depict the figures painted on the glass ovals.

SCALE describes how an object relates to some external measure such as a standard ruler or, in this case, another object. Compare the chest and writing table to each other. In terms of scale, one is short, one tall. One appears sturdy; the other lighter and more delicate.

❧

To understand the word *style* as merely a list of physical attributes, however, is too limiting. In order to comprehend fully the concept of style, it is important to move beyond the description of visual characteristics to investigate additional concepts, such as relationships and choice. The most obvious *relationships* are the connections among objects. One object might contain the same design element as another but in different materials. Thus, there is a relationship between a chair and a silver tray when both have ball-and-claw feet (figs. 3, 4). Or, parts of objects might be made in exactly the same way: two chests with identical drawer construction are related.

Left:
FIG. 3. Side chair

Below:
FIG. 4. Salver *(left)* and detail of salver *(right)*

Fig. 5. Desk-and-bookcase

Relationships can also exist between or among objects and aspects of the culture and society in which they were created. For example, a desk-and-bookcase made in the 1790s and decorated with an eagle finial and an inlaid eagle design (a patriotic symbol closely identified with the new nation) is an excellent example of an object that mirrors the values of the society in which it was created (fig. 5).

Choices about objects are made by both the makers and the buyers/users of those objects. Certain design elements or combinations of elements were created at particular times by individuals or groups of people for different reasons and to express different ideas. As in the example of the federal desk-and-bookcase, the choice of an eagle as the central decorative element was a deliberate one made by the craftsmen or by the person who ordered the desk or by the two in consultation.

Developing an appreciation for these three concepts—the visual characteristics, relationships, and choices inherent in any decorative art object—will lead to a better understanding of the concept of style. Yet an important question remains: Why do styles change? This is not an easy question; even the experts disagree on the reasons. Answering it requires thinking about how and why ideas permeate society, how trends develop, and why people make the choices they do.

New styles develop when people begin to stretch or change the limits of conventions. They look for new ways to achieve the same ends or identify and work toward completely new goals. In other words, they make different choices. Many factors cause such changes in choice: improvements in technology, the increasing or decreasing availability of materials, influences from other cultures, and changes in attitudes, to name only a few. The resulting changes may become accepted as part of an existing style or may result in the emergence of a new style.

Noted furniture historian Benno Forman believed that an additional force for change included the interaction of different groups who had distinct cultural traditions. Changes of this nature may be as subtle as an eighteenth-century Philadelphia cabinetmaker's adoption of a Germanic construction technique used by a local immigrant craftsman, or it may be as overt as the interaction of Pennsylvania Germans with people from the predominant English culture that results in the production of redware plates (a Pennsylvania German form) decorated with portraits of Lafayette and Washington (fig. 6).

Just as new influences affect people's stylistic choices, so too does the stability of a given culture, particularly a rural culture. Long after the style we now refer to as Chippendale swept into fashion in the port cities of Boston, New York,

FIG. 6. Redware plate

Philadelphia, and Williamsburg in the mid eighteenth century, cabinetmakers in smaller towns and rural areas continued to produce chairs in the familiar William and Mary and Queen Anne styles to satisfy local demand.

Even when the forces for change overcome those for stability, the change is seldom sudden. A single design element may change and become part of a new style. The introduction of the curved back in William and Mary–style chairs is a case in point. This new element was memorable and repeatable and worked well within the existing conventions, so craftsmen increasingly incorporated it as a feature in later William and Mary chairs. It was accepted as part of the prevailing taste or fashion (fig. 7). The curved back became part of a new style, one we now call Queen Anne (fig. 8), that included curved legs, a curved crest rail (the top of the seat back), and a vase-shape splat (the chair back).

Although the terms are often used interchangeably, *design* is not synonymous with *style*. A design is a plan for accomplishing a purpose. A person designs when he or she makes a plan (whether mental or physical), creates an object (such as a chair), or arranges and manipulates the things made by others (as in landscaping a garden, arranging an interior, or dressing for a party). We sometimes can discern a designer's purpose by carefully studying the result of his or her labors (whether

FIGS. 7 and 8. Side chairs

an object, a garden, or a room). In practice, a designer identifies a problem, such as the need for warm, comfortable clothing. To solve the problem, he or she may design a weave for a particular fabric. When faced with the desire to duplicate Asian lacquerwork, a furnituremaker developed a new technique, called japanning, that imitated this elaborate and expensive decoration. If the resulting design or effect is successful and is repeated frequently, it may become part of a new style.

Fashion, like *design*, is another term sometimes used interchangeably with *style*. Its meaning differs but in a more subtle, although no less important, way. A style may be in or out of fashion. A fashionable style is one that is dominant or popular among influential people and generally relates to a particular time, place, or group. Fashion can also dictate change for the sake of change and can cause people to buy objects for the sake of novelty or to remain "in fashion." But "fashion" is not limited to the dominant culture. On the contrary, some groups continued to prefer traditions fashionable in their former homelands. The Dutch settlers of the Hudson River valley, for example, continued to make and acquire the painted wardrobes that were popular in their homeland long after they had adapted other aspects of their culture to the predominant English fashions of their new home. The Shakers, a religious group that emigrated from England in the late eighteenth century, produced furniture, textiles, and drawings that reflected their religious beliefs. The simplicity of design, the functionality, and the superior construction of these objects also appealed to non-Shakers, who eagerly purchased the items and displayed them in their homes, launching a "fashion" for Shaker design.

Understanding a style is often easier than agreeing on what to call it. Authors of scholarly books and exhibition catalogues on the decorative arts generally use the stylistic terms that are most useful for the category of objects they are studying. For example, *rococo* (derived from a French term) might be the most useful word for discussing metal objects made in the third quarter of the eighteenth century, while *Chippendale* (the name of a designer) best describes the furniture of the same period, and *Georgian* is the term (derived from the English monarchy) that is most precise in describing the elegant town house in which these objects may have resided.

The names we use for various styles today often bear little or no relationship to how early Americans would have identified the objects surrounding them. Many of the most common names are products of the late nineteenth century, such as *Queen*

Anne. Other names, such as *Chippendale* or *Hepplewhite*, refer to a proponent of a given style. On the other hand, if we choose to use art historical terms such as *baroque* or *rococo*, we must face the difficulty of translating stylistic components from two-dimensional paintings to three-dimensional decorative arts objects.

Fortunately, what a style is called is less important than understanding the reasons why it has so many names. Understanding what objects in a certain style look like, why they look that way, and then calling them by a name that is commonly understood facilitates the study of our material past. For these reasons, we have chosen to use a mixture of names for the eight historical styles discussed in this book; these eight styles are frequently encountered at Winterthur and in today's antiques market.

It is not easy to accurately interpret the past, to understand why a style evolved and why it became popular or why it fell out of fashion. To fail to try, however, diminishes not only our ability to recognize a style but also our understanding of and appreciation for the people and the cultures that created it.

Fɪɢ. 9. From G. Charmeton, *Diverses ornemens pour servir à toutes sortes d'artisans* (Paris, 165?)

CHAPTER I

The Seventeenth-Century Style
FASHIONABLE BETWEEN 1620 AND 1680

Learning to Look

When the first English colonists landed along the Atlantic coast of North America in the seventeenth century, they carried with them more than a desire to start a new life or pursue economic opportunities in a land where their religious beliefs could be more freely expressed. From their old homes they brought household possessions and their ideas about design and craftsmanship. From the earliest days of settlement in New England in the 1620s to the last quarter of the seventeenth century, these possessions and ideas reflected the mannerist aesthetic, also known today as the seventeenth-century style. The seventeenth-century style in America, as practiced in the colonies, can be recognized by the abundance of ornamentation, predominant straight lines, and a liberal use of vibrant color.

ORNAMENTATION: A distinctive element of the seventeenth-century style is elaborate and intricate abstract decorative ornament. Mannerism in the European court tradition was characterized by an abundance of ornament, in particular, the use of classical imagery, such as urns, floral designs, and interwoven bands of decoration known as strapwork. Classical images in the seventeenth-century style were so elongated, distorted, and otherwise manipulated to fill space that the viewer often struggled to determine what the designs were supposed to represent. A plate (fig. 9) a seventeenth-century French design book epitomizes the mannerist love of intricate decoration. Note the interplay of twisted and curved decorative bands interspersed with human forms.

This same complexity of intertwined lines and shapes can be seen in a joined chest made in 1676 (fig. 10). The low-relief carving completely fills the front and sides of the chest but is contained within rigid, rectangular forms. The strapwork bands that frame the chest are likewise decorated with abstract palmette designs. Three recessed panels feature a series of S scrolls and highly stylized flowers in vase forms. The decorative design is complex, and all the elements relate seamlessly to one another. In addition, this chest exemplifies the straight line, right-angle construction of the seventeenth-century style. The form consists of elaborately

FIG. 10. Joined chest

FIG. 11. Drawer handle

carved panels fitted into a frame, demonstrating the highly compartmentalized approach characteristic of mannerist design.

The same aesthetic—decorative elements contained within a severe framework—can be seen in a brass drawer handle from a desk once owned by William Penn and preserved by nineteenth-century Philadelphia antiquarian John Fanning Watson (fig. 11). The handle is an escutcheon or, shield, in the form of a flower with four separate petals, each of which features another floral form framed within an arch. Like the decoration on the joined chest, the floral forms of the drawer handle are stylized and compartmentalized one within another.

LINE: The lines of seventeenth-century–style objects, both the overall outline and the bordered elements within a piece, are straight and join each other at right angles. This great chair is composed of a series of wooden members that are turned on a lathe and joined at right angles (fig. 12). The overall effect is one of rigidity and a boxlike appearance. The same emphasis on straight lines can also be seen in the joined chest (see fig. 10). This chair, although outwardly plain in appearance, also

Fig. 12. Armchair

reinforces the seventeenth-century love of ornamentation. Notice the lavish use of spindles on the chair, many of which are decorative rather than structural, as well as the subtle differences in turning patterns on the spindles and on the top and side posts and stretchers.

COLOR: Although time has robbed most seventeenth-century objects of the depth of their color, enough remains to justify the observation that seventeenth-century interiors were highly colorful. Bright red and blue paint decorated the front of the chest in figure 10. Vivid, multicolored textiles and ceramics, both imported and expensive, contributed to an overall sense of vitality in seventeenth-century living spaces. The portrait of a young woman, probably painted by late seventeenth-century artist Gerret Duyckinck, vibrates with color (fig. 13). Her left arm rests on a colorful "Turkey" carpet, whose design in bright blues and reds indicates that it may be an Ushak carpet (named for the region of Turkey where they were made), which were highly prized for their brightly colored patterns. The white lace surrounding her bodice and at the sleeves as well as the white flowers on her garment and white designs in the carpet unify the composition.

✌ How the Seventeenth-Century Style Became Fashionable

Mannerism refers to a style that developed in Italy in the sixteenth century after the Renaissance. Its influence spread northward through the royal courts of Spain and France and then into the Netherlands and took on aspects of each region's philosophy and politics. Lavish and costly design books were a principal method for transmitting knowledge of the style (see fig. 9). By the time mannerism reached England in the late sixteenth century, the style was much changed from its origins in the Papal courts of Rome and the European courts. Boldness and simplicity had replaced the more delicate and intricate designs of the court mannerist style. Thus, the mannerist tradition carried to North America by the people who emigrated from England reflected not the taste of royalty but that of a middle class.

Silver objects were easily shaped and manipulated and could emulate the grand sophistication of mannerist design. A caudle cup made by Robert Sanderson of Boston exhibits a complex and completely integrated mannerist design: the bulging sides of the cup echo the swell of the handles, which are formed as elongated,

Fig. 13. Portrait of an unknown woman

female-like figures known as caryatids (fig. 14). In ceramics, the same preference
for a relatively simple, uncomplicated line can be seen in this bottle for sack, a white
wine imported from Spain (fig. 15). Unlike the William and Mary style, which would
become fashionable after 1680 in the colonies, the seventeenth-century style did not
represent upper-class European taste.

❧ Living with Objects in the Seventeenth-Century Style

Inherent in the definition of style is the concept of *choice*. The objects that a seventeenth-century homeowner chose to live with not only reflected each homeowner's
style preferences but also revealed the limited choices available. Most settlers who
lived along the eastern seaboard in the late 1600s considered their homes well furnished if they possessed a bed, some chests for storage, a table, and perhaps a few
stools or benches, along with the necessary earthen- and wooden wares for cook-
ing, eating, and storing food. A 1668 inventory of the Massachusetts house of a relatively wealthy family lists a bed, a trundle bed, three storage pieces, and two chairs
in the parlor; the hall, or large living space, contained two old tables, two pieces of

FIG. 14. Caudle cup

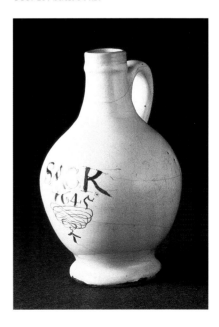

FIG. 15. Sack bottle

FIG. 16. Seventeenth-Century Room, Winterthur Museum (no longer on view)

seating furniture, and a box. Another bed, a table, and some seating furniture were upstairs. In short, the house contained little more than the necessities of life.

The room seen here displays the variety of objects that may have been available to a family in the seventeenth century (fig. 16). However, very few people would have owned so many expensive possessions, particularly the brass candlesticks and pewter plates on the table and the numerous furniture forms, including chairs, small tables, and a hanging cupboard. The most imposing possession of all would have been a joined cupboard, the large piece of furniture against the back wall. Intended more for display than storage, the cupboard dominates the room, not only due to its size but also because of the objects displayed on it representing the family's wealth. In addition, note the way in which the architecture itself reflects the seventeenth-century aesthetic with an emphasis on straight lines joined at right angles.

Textiles in the seventeenth century were exceedingly rare and expensive due both to the labor-intensive nature of their production and the fact that most were imported. Fortunate was the family that could drape its joined cupboard with a length of imported damask or invite a guest to sit on a chair with a cushion made of Turkey work, a textile created to imitate oriental carpets. Even rarer would have been a home displaying a silk quilt (fig. 17). Anyone entering the house would have perceived immediately the status and wealth of the family. Unlike the homey connotations surrounding quilts today, people in the seventeenth century regarded quilts as extremely exotic and the ultimate in luxury. This quilt embodies many of the same mannerist design elements as the seventeenth-century chest shown in figure 10. The design fills all available space with stitched patterns: in this case, a large ship framed by a ring of dogs, floral forms, medallions, and birds, all sur-

FIG. 17. Quilt

rounded by multiple borders. Like the carved designs on the chest, the quilt's design is complex and totally integrated.

Looking Ahead

By the 1680s a period of relative peace and prosperity began in England. This allowed the monarchy to turn its attention to its heretofore neglected American colonies. To shore up relations and solidify trade arrangements, a series of royal governors were sent to the colonies to oversee the interests of the new British rulers, William and Mary. The governors brought with them cargoes of household goods and new ideas that reflected a completely new approach to design. Known as baroque, this new aesthetic soon replaced the sturdy joined chest with a new form called a high chest and imposed elaborate ornamentation on such objects as silver tankards and ceramics.

Today, objects in the seventeenth-century style adorn only a few American homes. There is little demand for reproductions, and relatively few collectors seek out seventeenth-century–style furniture. Silver and ceramic objects in the mannerist style are collected and occasionally reproduced, but, for the most part, these items are rare. Therefore, it is easiest to learn about the style by visiting museums, such as the Museum of Fine Arts, Boston; and the Wadsworth Atheneum in Hartford, Connecticut; or the numerous historic houses and historical societies scattered along the East Coast, particularly in New England. There, the now-faded color palettes, the bulbous shapes, and the highly ornamental patterns stand as eloquent testimony to another world, one that social historian Peter Laslett refers to as "the world we have lost."

CHAPTER

2

The William and Mary Style

FASHIONABLE BETWEEN 1680 AND 1720

Learning to Look

*T*he William and Mary style, also known as early baroque, became popular in the British North American colonies around 1680 and remained in fashion throughout the first quarter of the eighteenth century, when it was replaced in popularity by a later version of the baroque aesthetic. The term *baroque* describes a style of decorative and fine art that is marked by strong diagonal, spiral, and curved lines and the dramatic interplay of light and dark, or highlight and shadow, across surfaces.

Named after the English monarchs who popularized it, the William and Mary style is most easily recognized by an emphasis on the vertical line and a unity of structure (particularly in furniture), with lavish decorative ornamentation based on curved lines, robust textures, and contrasting colors.

LINE: William and Mary–style objects are emphatically vertical, with abundant straight lines and elongated proportions. Notice that the height of the armchair is more than double the width and almost double the depth (fig. 18). The verticality is emphasized by the straight rather than curved structural elements. Although structurally similar to the broad, turned great chairs of the seventeenth century (see fig. 12), William and Mary–style chairs are distinctly more vertical.

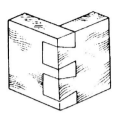

Detail drawing
showing a dovetail

FIG. 18. Armchair

ORNAMENTATION: The highly figured burl walnut and maple veneer gives this high chest an elaborate appearance and showcases the characteristic baroque light and dark contrast (fig. 19). The variation of color invites the eye to move up and down and over the front of the chest. The design also encourages the eye to move upward along the slender trumpet-turned legs and the "stepped-in" relationship of the bottom to the top half of the chest. The key to William and Mary–style ornament is in its close integration with the form of the object. Curved lines abound in the

FIG. 19. High chest

undulating stretchers, in the multi-arched outline on the skirt of the lower case piece, in the controlled turnings of the legs, and in the swirl of the burled veneer. Yet the curves are contained within the essentially vertical outline of the object. Like the chair, the chest is taller than it is wide or deep. It is constructed with a wood-working technique known as dovetailing, which was introduced in America by London-trained craftsmen. Dovetails allowed cabinetmakers to more easily produce lighter and taller cases, which could then be covered with decorative veneers.

TEXTURE: The fairly complex composition of contrasting curves of this drawer pull has been further enhanced with carved/incised flower and beading motifs across its surface (fig. 20). Metalworkers, particularly silversmiths, working in the William and Mary style favored decorative motifs such as elaborate floral decorations and figurative masks. These deeply textured surfaces reflect light and harbor shadows, creating visually exciting surfaces in the William and Mary style.

COLOR: Much like the high chest with its highly figured veneers, paintings in the William and Mary style feature sharp contrasts in hue and value. In this portrait of Magdalena Douw, a young American woman of Dutch descent, the elaborate brocade gown and the Turkey carpet on which her arm rests are alive with rich, deeply saturated colors (fig. 21). Notice the way in which color is used to move your eye over the painting: from the bright red of the shoes to the book in her right hand to the bunch of cherries held in the other to the red band encircling her cap. From the cap, your eye picks out the touches of white: to the lace framing her bodice and the deep ruffles at her sleeves and back to the white trim on the red shoes. Then your eye

FIG. 20. Drawer handle

Opposite:
FIG. 21. Portrait of
Magdalena Douw (Gansevoort)

moves upward again, following the blue spiral design in Magdalena's skirt to the blue bows on her bodice and then out the window to the blue hills and sky beyond. The open windows that frame her figure provide the strong light that contrasts with the dark tones of the interior and with the blue-greens of Magdalena's lavish gown. Painters of the baroque era perfected this technique of using contrasting light and dark tones in their work to create a sense of movement and drama.

❧ How the William and Mary Style Became Fashionable

The name *William and Mary* honors two British monarchs and reflects the changing political circumstances of the colonies after the early years of settlement. In 1689 William of Orange, chief magistrate of the United Provinces of the Netherlands, and his cousin and wife, Mary, accepted the invitation of the English Parliament to rule England. When the new monarchs established themselves at the English court, they brought with them a design tradition from the Netherlands that blended many elements, most notably from three sources: Dutch, Asian, and French.

The Dutch influence has its roots in Spain and the close connections between two realms of the Hapsburg monarchy. The Asian influence was already well established in the English court due to the marriage, in 1662, of the newly restored Stuart Monarch, Charles II, to Catherine of Braganza, a Portuguese princess who brought to her marriage her home country's trade connections, which included India and China. By the end of the seventeenth century, brightly colored, painted Indian cottons dominated the European market not only because they were inexpensive and lightweight but also because their colorful, highly figurative designs captivated the European imagination. The design of this bedspread, or *palampore*, as it was called at the time, fills every available space with scrolling tendrils and flowers (fig. 22).

British interest in luxury goods from the Far East increased in the middle years of the seventeenth century. Popular imports included silks, spices, and teas and tea wares, particularly fine porcelains. Although Europeans would not possess the secret for making true porcelain for another century, they enthusiastically embraced the shapes and forms of imported Chinese porcelain as well as the custom of drinking tea. A new market flourished for earthenwares and stonewares that were shaped and decorated to imitate the Chinese designs.

French influence can be traced to the designs of Daniel Marot, who fled the French court to settle for a time in Holland, where his talents served William and

FIG. 22. Bedspread

Mary. He would later follow the monarchs to England, arriving there by 1689. This looking glass was brought to the colonies by Pieter Schuyler, a New York landholder, following a trip to the English court in 1709 or 1710 (fig. 23). Its form and decoration are typical of Marot's designs, and it illustrates the strong verticality and exuberant ornament of the William and Mary style, including the human face, or mask, that decorates the center bottom. With its featherlike headdress, the head may represent the European perception of Native American dress and, as such, reflects the European fascination with people and places considered exotic.

Fig. 23. Looking glass

Opposite:

Fig. 24. Flock Room, Winterthur Museum

Thus, although the name may be misleading, it is clear that the William and Mary style represented a truly international phenomenon. In a short time evidences of the new style found their way to the North American colonies. William and Mary sent royal governors to the colonies to strengthen British influence, and these agents of the Crown brought with them the new design influences in the form of English household furnishings and craftsmen.

❧ Living with Objects in the William and Mary Style

One of the hallmarks of the William and Mary style was the development of unified interior design schemes. Daniel Marot was one of the first designers to view a
room as a unified whole. His prints influenced not only the designs of individual
objects but also the careful arrangement of objects within a room. Woodwork,
painted decoration, furniture, textile hangings, upholstery, and even Chinese porcelains (displayed in carefully designed wall mounts) all contributed to a room's overall effect.

Designed rooms featured suites of matching furniture, including sets of chairs
and companion high chests and dressing tables. Objects were carefully arranged on
tabletops, and textiles and decorative accessories were deliberately chosen to contribute to the appearance of the room as a whole. The high wings of the easy chair
and the flowing designs in the wallpaper of this room at Winterthur show clearly
the strong curves that dominate ornament in the William and Mary style (fig. 24).
Highlights glint off the rounded surfaces of spiral-turned table legs and fireplace

andirons—examples of the baroque interest in the play of light and shadow over bold, three-dimensional surfaces.

Tables made specifically for the service of tea appear in inventories for the first time during the heyday of the William and Mary style. The custom of drinking tea and accumulating the accessories of a well-stocked tea table became popular pursuits during the eighteenth century. The colonies emerged as a ready market for imported tea, and foreign manufacturers were quick to supply the glass, silver, and ceramic vessels necessary for the proper observance of this social ritual (fig. 25). Wealthy families could afford to impress their visitors with elaborate and up-to-date objects such as this sugar box made by Edward Winslow of Boston (fig. 26). The bold three-dimensionality of the decoration creates areas of highlight and shadow when light plays across its surface.

FIG. 25. Earthenware teapot

FIG. 26. Silver sugar box

Despite the fact that objects in the William and Mary style became widely available in the colonies by the early eighteenth century, this newest style remained very
much an upper-class phenomenon and did not trickle down in any substantial
degree to the middle or lower classes. For the majority of colonists, who were nei-
ther city dwellers nor wealthy, the new style exerted little influence. Most owned
very few objects; fewer still owned the land that they worked in this predominantly
agricultural economy. Therefore, the only contact that many had with the William
and Mary style was through the purchase of affordable, locally produced, utilitar-
ian chairs.

❧ Looking Ahead

By the 1720s, the popularity of the early baroque aesthetic had begun to wane in the
colonies. Following the lead of the tastemakers in England and on the Continent,

colonists came to prefer a later version of the baroque, one that put greater emphasis on curved forms that were not contained within rectilinear frames. Unlike other
furniture styles that were to undergo revivals in the nineteenth century, the William
and Mary style never regained its popularity. Even today, it is, in the words of one
scholar, seldom studied and little known. Nonetheless, the co-mingling of design
influences in the style—Asian, French, Dutch, and English—lead many to consider
it the first truly international style. As such, the exuberant curves and elaborately
decorated objects designed in the William and Mary style serve as accurate reflec-
tions of an age that witnessed great expansion—expansion in knowledge of the
known world, in scientific discoveries, and in trade. It was a time that historians
often refer to as "The Age of Discovery."

CHAPTER

The Queen Anne Style
FASHIONABLE BETWEEN 1720 AND 1755

Learning to Look

𝒯he Queen Anne style, also referred to as late baroque or Georgian, became fashionable in the colonies around 1720 and remained in vogue through the 1750s, when the exuberance of the French rococo style surpassed it in popularity. The Queen Anne style is a blend of several influences, including baroque, classical, Continental, and Asian. It draws on the William and Mary style through its emphasis on line, proportion, and balance. The major differences between an early baroque, or William and Mary–style object, and a late baroque, or Queen Anne–style object, lies in the degree of elaboration of the curved line, in the emphasis on overall form, and in the interplay of solids and voids. Named in the nineteenth century for the last Stuart Queen of England, who reigned from 1702 to 1714, the Queen Anne style is most easily recognized by the emphasis on the curved line, which becomes the outline of the object; its strict adherence to classical proportions; and the restrained use of ornamentation and color.

LINE: Curved lines define the Queen Anne style. Not only are the overall outlines of Queen Anne objects ensembles of curves, but each individual element is also based on curves. This Boston chair represents an early version of the style as it first appeared in the colonies in the second quarter of the eighteenth century (fig. 27).

Note the curved cabriole leg (in the period it was called "horsebone"), the vase-shape splat (in the chair back), the compass-shape seat, the pad feet, and the yoke-shape crest rail (the top of the chair back). All of these elements are curved and relate to one another in a unifying way. Even the back legs curve outward. Although later versions of this type of chair would be more curvilinear, especially chairs made in Philadelphia, the essential elements of the Queen Anne style are all in place in this chair.

Fig. 27. Side chair

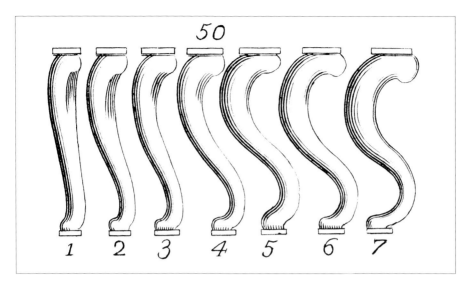

F<small>IG</small>. 28. From William Hogarth, *The Analysis of Beauty* (London: Printed for Samuel Bagster, [1810]), detail of plate B

The extent and degree to which a line should curve was not a random choice for designers and artists in the eighteenth century. William Hogarth, noted British artist and art critic, published a treatise entitled *The Analysis of Beauty* in 1753 in which he identified the ideal line of beauty. He claimed that not just any curved line met the definition of "ideal." In this illustration from Hogarth's book, the proclaimed ideal degree of curvature is number 4 (fig. 28).

P<small>ROPORTION</small>: The influence of classicism on the Queen Anne style is manifested in a firm control of proportion. Proportion is the relationship of one part of an object to another and is usually based on complex mathematical formulas. For example, the various parts of this well-proportioned high chest relate to one another in precise ways: the height of the chest is almost twice the width, whereas the depth is one-half the width (fig. 29). In large part the emphasis on proportion in Queen Anne–style furniture derived from Renaissance precedents. By 1715 an English translation of Andrea Palladio's *Four Books of Architecture* was widely available. Palladio, a Renaissance architect, developed formulas for determining proper proportions—whether for buildings, rooms, or furniture—based on ancient Roman precedents. This approach to design, today known as Palladian, first achieved great popularity in the second quarter of the eighteenth century.

ORNAMENTATION: Unlike the early baroque, or William and Mary style, or the rococo, which would supplant it in popularity, the later baroque, or Queen Anne style, featured relatively little ornamentation. Small cabriole legs composed of lions' faces and paw feet and the acorn finial are the only decorative elements on this extremely rare glass teapot (fig. 30). The teapot's shape is its most striking characteristic, from the gracefully globular form of the body to the looped handle and gently curved spout. Compare the design of this teapot with figure 25 in the William and Mary chapter. The dominant visual characteristic in that earthenware teapot is its applied ornamentation, while in the Queen Anne–style teapot, the curved line is more important than any applied decorative feature.

In Queen Anne–style furniture, simple scallop shells, sometimes delicately highlighted with gilt, and architectural features such as pediments and fluted columns are often the only ornament added to the basic form of a chair, chest, or tea table. The one exception to the subdued use of ornamentation in the Queen Anne style is japanning, a technique developed in the West to imitate Asian lacquerwork. A rural craftsman in Connecticut produced this exuberant high chest, which incorporates an exaggerated version of the fashionable curved leg as well as exotic japanned decoration (fig. 31). Japanning involved painting the surface of an object either black or red and then applying layers of gesso (a plasterlike substance) to create the fanciful figures imitating Chinese designs.

Opposite:
FIG. 29. High chest
FIG. 30. Glass teapot

Fɪɢ. 31. High chest

Cᴏʟᴏʀ: Another defining characteristic of the Queen Anne style is the restrained use of color. Preferring the curved line over applied ornamentation, craftsmen making fashionable objects in the later baroque era often rejected highly figured veneers and elaborately gilded or highly painted surfaces, preferring instead smooth, flat surfaces and a restrained color palette. The portrait of Mrs. Charles Willing, painted by Robert Feke, one of the colonies' first native-born portrait painters, is a study in soft neutral colors (fig. 32). Mrs. Willing's dress, in grayish-brown tones, is set off by white lace at the neckline and sleeves. The landscape depicted by Feke in the background is equally restrained: predominantly soft browns, greens, and blues. The

Fig. 32. *Mrs. Charles Willing (Anne Shippen)*

FIG. 33. Bedcover

exception, again, comes from the East. Colorful Indian textiles and particularly inexpensive painted and resist-dyed cottons swept the European market (fig. 33). Despite the different use of color, there are similarities in the patterns of Mrs. Willing's dress and the Indian textile—both emphasize curving, foliate designs in an intricate, dense pattern.

❧ How the Queen Anne Style Became Fashionable

The era that ushered in the popularity of the Queen Anne style began auspiciously with the signing of the Treaty of Utrecht in 1713, a treaty that ended almost one hundred years of conflict between France and other Western powers, most notably England. With peace came prosperity, and fortunes were quickly made in the newly opened trading routes to the Far East. The influence of Asian design traditions, first seen in the West in the late seventeenth century, grew stronger in the first half of the eighteenth century. Thanks in part to increased trade with the East, Asian goods were more readily available, and Western artisans eagerly adopted many of their design features, including vase-shape chair backs, the bowed curve, and, possibly, the ball-and-claw foot. Brass hardware also reflected Asian forms, as evidenced in this furniture pull shaped like an abstract moth or bat wing (fig. 34), both popular forms in oriental design. As noted above, objects in the Queen Anne style continued not only the baroque emphasis on the curved line but also an adherence to clas-

FIG. 34. Cabinet handle on a desk-and-bookcase

sical proportions. In addition, the influence of Continental traditions, in particular Dutch designs, is especially apparent in furniture forms that emphasize contrasting curves, most notably the S curve of the cabriole leg. The hoof foot (so named because it resembles an animal hoof) and the swelled fronts of desks-and-bookcases also are attributable to Dutch influence.

Further development of regional craft traditions occurred in the early eighteenth century. Artisans in major urban or regional centers in America were influenced by the craftsmen who trained them, by the artisans who worked alongside them, and by those who worked in nearby shops. Craftsmen chose to work in ways and to produce designs that were practical and successful in their market area; in other words, they prospered if they produced objects in the forms and with the designs their customers wanted. Therefore a tankard crafted by a silversmith in Boston differed in shape and volume from one made in New York during the same time period; this, in turn, differed from the product of a Philadelphia craftsman (fig. 35). These differences may be obvious or subtle, but they are readily apparent to someone who has trained his or her eye to look carefully. The tankard made in Boston

From left to right:
FIG. 35. Boston, Philadelphia, and New York tankards

(left) is tall and tapered with a finial on the lid; the tankard made in New York *(right)* features a short, broad body with a scalloped edge on the lid. In contrast to both, the tankard made in Philadelphia *(center)* has a swelled, or "bellied," body. All exemplify the Queen Anne style, but their differences reflect the distinctive, prevailing taste of the region in which they were made.

The Queen Anne style, then, represents a well-integrated blending of several design influences in the early eighteenth century, thanks to a respite in Europe from constant wars and an improved economic climate. It retains the baroque attention to overall form but is marked by an emphasis on the curved line, particularly on contrasting curves. Craftsmen working in the style used the classical system of proportion for the overall appearance of an object and easily integrated Asian design elements into both the form and the decoration of objects.

❧ *Living with Objects in the Queen Anne Style*

Inventories from the eighteenth century demonstrate that people at almost all economic levels lived more comfortably than their counterparts of the previous century. They built larger and better-constructed homes and furnished them with a greater variety of goods, many of which had previously been luxuries available only to the very wealthy. Silver teaspoons; pewter plates; ceramic mugs and bowls; delicate, stemmed wineglasses; and an array of new furniture forms were now within the reach of a growing number of people. In sum, many people living at this time had more choice and greater comfort.

The elegant eighteenth-century home also featured many relatively new furniture forms: desks, tea tables, corner chairs, couches, and chests of drawers. All were considered essential for living in an elegant manner. During the eighteenth century, a new emphasis on comfort led to an increase in the production of upholstered chairs and couches. The most dramatic reflection of this new interest was found in the bedchamber. Elaborately furnished beds with canopies and with bed hangings made from expensive, imported fabrics, such as chintz, silk, and wool, became more common among the wealthy. Wooden bedsteads to hold these lavish bed furnishings replaced simple straw pallets that were laid directly on the floor, and other items, such as mirrors, chests of drawers, closed stools (a chair that holds a chamber pot), and easy chairs, became more readily available. While people continued

FIG. 36. Cecil Bedroom, Winterthur Museum

to put their best bed in a parlor, they placed new emphasis on the bedchamber as a separate place to receive and entertain visitors, hence the need for high-quality furnishings and additional seating forms (fig. 36).

With the increased popularity of the social custom of tea drinking, the parlor became a focal point of the home. Tea parties, both for the immediate family as well as for invited guests, became more common in England during the reign of Queen Anne, and their popularity spread to the colonies. Tea drinking required not only a knowledge of the etiquette surrounding the ritual but also possession of the wide range of proper accessories; cups, teapots, waste bowls, sugar tongs, saucers, spoons, and creamers all adorned a well-dressed tea table. Taking tea became more than a welcome break at the end of an afternoon or evening; it assumed the role of social arbiter, separating those who knew how to properly pour and drink tea from those who did not.

❧ Looking Ahead

The Queen Anne style remained popular in the colonies long after it had fallen out of favor in England. As late as the end of the eighteenth century, objects best identified as Queen Anne were still made in both urban and rural workshops in America. However, for those Americans with a taste for the very latest fashion and the pocketbook to support their taste, the preference for the late baroque design exemplified by the Queen Anne style had given way to a preference for the fanciful, and often frivolous, designs of the rococo, or Chippendale, style.

Few styles have retained their popularity over a longer period of time than the style known today as Queen Anne. Whether browsing through an antiques store or modern furnishings emporium or thumbing through the pages of a home furnishings magazine, shoppers are repeatedly attracted to objects made in the Queen Anne style. The gracefully flowing lines of a tea table; the soft curve of a silver teapot; or the simple, branching tree-of-life design on a piece of upholstery fabric exemplify the style's timeless appeal.

The Chippendale Style

FASHIONABLE BETWEEN 1755 AND 1790

Learning to Look

*T*he Chippendale style, named somewhat erroneously after English cabinetmaker Thomas Chippendale, became popular in the colonies around 1755 and remained in fashion until 1790, when the cessation of the war with England once again opened up the ports of the new nation to English goods in the latest classical taste. For the most part, objects in the Chippendale style retain the emphasis on balance and proportion so prevalent in the Queen Anne style. What was new in this style, however, was the extensive use of ornament, including delicate and fanciful shells; rocaille (rock formations); ruffled-edge acanthus leaves (known as raffles); and sinuous, asymmetrical, pierced patterns (fig. 37). This ornament is more accurately referred to as rococo, a reference to a design movement popular in France in the early eighteenth century. In addition, objects in the Chippendale style favored a more vertical, as opposed to curved, emphasis in line and often broke away from the strict symmetry of the early eighteenth century in favor of unbalanced arrangements in ornamentation and design. The Chippendale style is most easily recognized by its lavish ornamentation, the use of vertical lines to outline furniture forms, asymmetrical decorative elements, and contrasting textures.

FIG. 37. High chest

Fig. 38. Salver

ORNAMENTATION: The liberal use of surface ornamentation is perhaps the primary identifier of objects in the Chippendale style. The high chest in figure 37 incorporates abundant ornament typical of the period: floral motifs, rosettes, ruffles, and naturalistic foliate carving. The pediment forms the most distinctive aspect of this high chest: superimposed on the classical pediment are purely rococo decorative elements. Elaborate vegetation drips from colonettes while the cartouche (the topmost, central, elaborately decorated element) features lavish asymmetrical carving. No exact prototype for this design is known, and it would appear to be a free interpretation based on the designs of Englishmen Thomas Chippendale and Thomas Johnson rather than an exact copy from any one source. The depth of the carvings, the highly figured mahogany surface with a vibrant grain pattern, and the elaborate brasses all contribute to the decorative appearance. The overall effect is one of movement and vitality.

The same use of surface ornamentation can be seen on a salver, or tray, made by New York silversmith John Heath bearing the Schuyler family coat of arms (fig. 38). A central cartouche, surrounded by typical rococo floral and leaf decoration, also includes a falcon perched atop a knight's helmet as well as an identical falcon inside the cartouche. In addition, the gadrooned border of the salver and the ruffled decorative band inside the gadrooning both represent a restrained American interpretation of the rococo aesthetic.

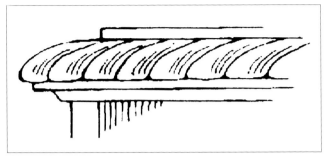

Example of gadrooning

Fig. 39. Side chair

LINE: In America, fanciful rococo ornament was balanced by the straight lines of the classical elements that colonial craftsmen were apt to use in their work. Quarter-round pilasters resembling temple columns (seen on the high chest) marked the corners of high chests made in the Chippendale style, and the pediment was a classically inspired architectural feature decorated with the asymmetrical rococo ornament popular with consumers.

Although objects in the Chippendale style retain the curved, or cabriole, leg of the Queen Anne style, the rest of the object emphasizes the vertical. Notice the straight stiles and trapezoidal-shape seat on this Philadelphia side chair (fig. 39). The vertical line is further reinforced through the use of an elongated figure-eight design in the back splat. However, the interlaced strapwork employs an asymmetrical line as does the elaborate carving on the knees.

TEXTURE: The Chippendale style often presents a study in contrasting textures, as seen in this cabinet handle (fig. 40). Intricate sculptured designs, inspired by the Chinese taste, contrast with the smooth metallic surface of the brass. Notice also the lavish use of both the rococo and Chinese design elements: C scrolls, ruffles, columns, and floral forms from the rococo; and the pagoda roof and cross-hatched designs from the Chinese. The textured surface of this redware teapot was created

FIG. 40. Cabinet handle on a desk-and-bookcase

FIG. 41. Redware teapot

from an elaborate rococo design carved into a mold used to make the teapot (fig. 41). In addition, the sheep finial is also finely textured. Other characteristics of the rococo style can be seen here as well: the asymmetrical placement of the rococo design on the body of the pot and the use of a straight rather than curved spout.

❧ How the Chippendale Style Became Fashionable

The Chippendale style reached the colonies by the mid eighteenth century in three forms: in widely disseminated design books published in England; in the minds and work habits of craftsmen who immigrated to America from Great Britain; and in designs of imported objects. One of the most influential books was Thomas Chippendale's *Gentleman and Cabinet-Maker's Director* (fig. 42). This plate is one of six featuring chair designs from the 1754 edition. Chippendale published designs for many furniture forms, including bookcases, writing tables, breakfast tables, and dressing and china tables as well as shelves, firescreens, and clock cases. Chippendale intended his book to help a gentleman make his choice and to help the cabinetmaker execute it. He provided detailed, illustrated instructions for the

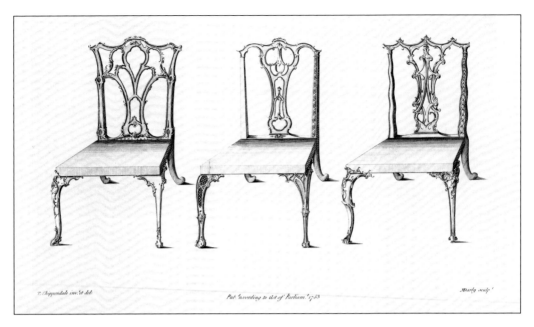

FIG. 42. Chair designs. From Thomas Chippendale, *The Gentleman and Cabinet-Maker's Director* (London: By the author, 1754), plate 15

correct proportions of a chair, for example, and then enlarged the decorative design for the chair back so the proportions would remain correct.

On the left chair in this drawing, the top center of the crest rail shows the C curves and rufflelike rocaille that are characteristic of what Chippendale called the "modern," or "French," taste. On the center chair, the pointed arch, characteristic of what Chippendale termed the "Gothic" taste, decorates the lower center of the splat (the center of the chair back), and the carving on the top of the right leg. The pagoda-like decorations on the crest rail of the chair on the right evoke the Chinese taste. In the cabinet handle noted above (see fig. 40), a central pagoda and the fret-work underneath it are paired with foliate elements on either side, a prime example of the way in which Chinese design motifs were incorporated into various objects in the Chippendale style.

Influential cabinetmakers or architects who owned copies of the *Director* included John Goddard of Newport, Rhode Island; Thomas Affleck of Philadelphia; William Buckland of Annapolis; and Thomas Jefferson of Virginia. Other important printed design sources included Abraham Swan's *British Architect* and Robert

Manwaring's *Cabinet and Chair-Maker's Real Friend and Companion*. What is important to note is that few, if any, objects were exact re-creations of English designs. Rather, American craftsmen felt free to borrow elements at will or combine them in unique patterns.

Objects imported into the colonies from Britain either for personal use or to be sold for profit formed another important means of style transmission. This quilted cotton bedspread exemplifies the way in which the Chippendale style combined elements of the chinoiserie, or Chinese-influenced design, with the rococo (fig. 43). Fanciful Chinese figures enliven the print while naturalistic foliate forms spread across the fabric in random fashion.

But by far the most influential factor in the arrival of the Chippendale style was the immigration of craftsmen from Europe into the colonies. Between the 1750s and

FIG. 43. Quilt

1760s, many highly skilled craftsmen, including engravers, silversmiths, and cabinetmakers, arrived in America and settled in the major cities that were home to the wealthy patrons essential for the support of their trades. Silversmiths such as Daniel Christian Fueter and Phillip Syng Jr. were immigrants from Switzerland and Ireland respectively, while Paul Revere in Boston, Myer Myers in New York, and Joseph Richardson Jr. in Philadelphia were second-generation immigrants. In furniture, Philadelphia became home to a highly skilled group of English carvers that included Thomas Affleck, Nicholas Bernard, Martin Jugiez, and Hercules Courtenay. Among them, they produced the purest manifestation of rococo design in the colonies.

❧ Living with Objects in the Chippendale Style

The rococo era in the colonies introduced greater material wealth and luxury consumption than had been previously known. Highly carved and decorated furniture, luxurious fabrics, polished leather, sparkling crystal, and delicate ceramics adorned the homes of the wealthy, as seen in the Blackwell Parlor at Winterthur (fig. 44). Perhaps the premier example of this new wealth was the three-story town house of John Cadwalader, located near the docks of the Delaware River, within blocks of the building now known as Independence Hall. Cadwalader's fortune grew out of his lucrative investments in the merchant ships that sailed from the colonies to London and the West Indies. His marriage to wealthy Maryland heiress Elizabeth Lloyd solidified his position as one of the wealthiest colonists of his day. The couple filled their town house with the fruits of their wealth; elaborately carved chairs, mantelpieces, card and pier tables, mirrors, and silver objects flowed in from the workshops of famed Philadelphia carvers and silversmiths. They imported from abroad only what could not be obtained in Philadelphia, in particular luxury textiles and fine carpets.

Not everyone lived in a style comparable to the Cadwalader's, but more Americans were able to furnish their homes with a small sampling of luxury items both locally made and imported. They also adopted the genteel pastimes associated with these objects, including drinking tea, playing card games, and having a por-

Fɪɢ. 44. Blackwell Parlor, Winterthur Museum

FIG. 45. *Mrs. Benjamin Rush (Julia Stockton)*

trait painted. Mrs. Benjamin Rush, born Julia Stockton, sat for her portrait at the time of her wedding to Dr. Rush in 1776 (fig. 45). Noted Philadelphia painter Charles Willson Peale captured the essence of the age in the lush fabric of the blue dress and in the rust-colored drapery trimmed with fringe in the left background. Note the way in which Peale's composition exemplifies the characteristics of the Chippendale style in the opposed C curves of Rush's inclined neck and bent arm and the delicacy and naturalism of the lace and foliage at her neck. Objects in the Chippendale style such as this painting echoed the emergence of new wealth and a preference for luxury goods in pre-Revolutionary America.

❧ Looking Ahead

Through the publication of his design book, Thomas Chippendale achieved widespread fame in his own time and beyond. The name *Chippendale* is significant for two reasons: (1) it was the first style to be disseminated widely through design books; and (2) of the styles discussed in this book, it is the only one that bears a commoner's name and that became fashionable in the colonies through the patronage of commoners.

Objects in the Chippendale style represent gentility; they present an image of strong leadership by wealthy, educated, and responsible men, perhaps explaining why interest in Chippendale-style furnishings has resurfaced many times since it first became fashionable in the late 1700s. A wave of nostalgia and national pride surrounding the one-hundredth anniversary of the Declaration of Independence in 1876 prompted many Americans to collect antique furnishings and to buy reproductions inspired by the Chippendale style. This interest, called the colonial revival by twentieth-century scholars, lasted for several decades. Even today Chippendale-style furnishings and decorative objects, reminders of that crucial period in American history, continue to be produced and purchased.

No sooner had the Chippendale style and the rococo design aesthetic been embraced in the colonies, however, than English advocates of the classical taste, such as Scottish architect Robert Adam, began designing rooms and furnishings for people at the highest levels of English society. These new classical designs were inspired by archaeological excavations in Italy and were made popular in England through the printed design books of Thomas Sheraton and George Hepplewhite. Following the Revolutionary War, the classical style quickly became accessible to merchants, tradesmen, and small landowners, just as Chippendale's designs had two decades earlier. Leaders in the new United States worked to strengthen the country's economy and government after the disruptions of war and to establish a stable, federal form of government under the first president, George Washington. During these formative years for the new nation, many people turned away from Chippendale's designs to embrace the new classical designs and unite them with patriotic imagery, creating a style we now call federal.

CHAPTER

The Federal Style

FASHIONABLE BETWEEN 1790 AND 1815

Learning to Look

*T*he federal, or early classical revival, style became popular in the new United States following the Revolutionary War and remained in fashion into the nineteenth century. It was replaced around 1815 by the more archaeologically correct empire, or later classical revival, style. Inspired by the excavations taking place at the ancient Roman cities of Herculaneum and Pompeii, manifestations of this new style came to be known collectively as classical; however, there was no single approach to its expression. Many countries adapted classicism to reflect their recent history. The French added classical elements to their highly developed rococo style, creating a thoroughly French interpretation of classical design that was referred to by the name of the then-reigning monarch, Louis XVI. In England the style came to be referred to in terms relating to its leading proponents—namely, Robert Adam, a distinguished architect whose travels to Italy and subsequent drawings of its architecture and interiors contributed to intense interest in antiquity. Thomas Sheraton and George Hepplewhite also published design books of furniture that popularized Adam's work. In the United States the style became firmly tied to the spirit of the New Republic, hence the name *federal*. But whether it is called early classical revival, Louis XVI, Adam, Sheraton, Hepplewhite, or federal, all versions of the style share certain distinct characteristics: delicate scale, straight lines, vibrant colors, smooth textures, classical proportions, and classical ornamentation used in inlay, printed, and painted decoration.

LINE: The line of federal-style objects is often very straight and meets at right angles. Curves appear less frequently, sometimes relegated to shield-shape chair backs or the delicate arabesque designs on textiles and wallpaper. This New York sideboard is essentially a rectangular box supported by eight barely tapered legs (fig. 46). The severity of the sideboard's form is relieved, however, by the understated curves along the front: the front face of the sideboard sweeps in and out, giving the object a sense of movement and dynamism.

An interplay of geometric shapes in contrasting veneers also figures prominently in federal-period design. In this sideboard, the inlaid decoration features an array of geometric shapes; rectangles softened by curved ends (often referred to as an "astragal-end") and ovals outlined with inlay grace the drawer fronts, while larger ovals differentiated by highly figured veneers enliven the cabinet fronts. Notice the close interplay of geometric shapes: squares segmented into vertical rectangles and ovals within rectangles and squares. The sideboard presents a linear appearance

FIG. 46. Sideboard

FIG. 47. Side chair

while, at the same time, forcing the eye to move along the many curved surfaces. All in all, this object epitomizes federal design.

SCALE AND VOLUME: Objects in the federal style present the appearance of lightness and delicacy. The incurving back legs of this side chair, combined with slender, tapered front legs as well as the simple, open design of the back splat all contribute to the overall effect of lightness (fig. 47). Probably made in Philadelphia in the late eighteenth century, the chair's deep brownish-black color is offset by brightly painted decorative elements, including fruit, flowers, and ostrich plumes tied neatly with a six-loop ribbon.

ORNAMENTATION: Classical motifs, including urns, swags, paterae (an oval shape derived from ancient, two-handled drinking vessels), volutes (ram's-horn scrolls), acanthus leaves, and husks are just some of the design elements that decorate the surfaces of federal-style objects. This print of George Washington exhibits a full array of federal ornamentation (fig. 48). Washington's bust was a popular subject for printmakers at the time the federal style was popular. Here it is framed in an oval surmounted by a leafy swag. The plinth (the square base of a column or pedestal) that supports the oval frame is surrounded by a panoply, or pile, of objects. The panoply has its origins in the ancient Greek celebration of a military victory; following a victory, the warriors would heap the arms of the defeated enemy at the base of a tree. Note that the forms in this panoply—a drum, banners, and eighteenth-century weapons of war—are indicative of Washington's military career and reflect the patriotism of the federal era.

COLOR: The federal color palette favored vibrant colors. Recent studies in paint analysis have shown that people in this era often painted their walls in deep tones

FIG. 48. *His Excell\cy George Washington, Esq\r*

FIG. 49. Bedspread

of blue, green, and red. An echo of this fondness for deeply saturated colors can also be seen in the popular painted furniture of the federal era (see fig. 47). Color was not limited to painted decoration, however; it also appears in the sharply contrasting woods in inlaid decoration, in the liberal application of gilt and gold leaf decoration, and in brightly colored textiles. John Hewson, the first known calico printer in Pennsylvania, produced this lively bedspread sometime in the late eighteenth century (fig. 49). The vibrant reds, pinks, and greens of the design are set off sharply by the gold and brown tones in the border. The design itself reflects many aspects of the federal style, including a central urn encased in a central square which, in turn, is framed in a larger rectangle, as well as an abundance of delicate, decorative forms including flowers, birds, and butterflies.

TEXTURE: Objects in the federal style feature smooth surfaces with very little three-dimensional applied decoration. The smooth, flat surfaces of furniture, the transfer-printed decoration on flat ceramic bodies, and the increased popularity of mirrors all combined to give the federal style a reflective quality. In silver objects especially, this emphasis on flat, reflective surfaces is elegantly manifested (fig. 50). Technological advances began to influence the production of silver in the late eighteenth century. This is most readily evident in the production of smooth sheets of silver through the use of hand-powered rolling mills. Such sheets of silver were perfectly suited to the classical forms popular in the federal style and were an ideal base for the delicate engraving, applied beading, and pierced galleries (open-work

FIG. 50. Silver tea and coffee service

FIG. 51. Stoneware teapot

decoration). Notice how the various components of this silver set also reflect the federal interest in the interplay of geometric shapes: the sugar bowl, waste bowl, and creamer feature circular stems resting on square bases.

PROPORTION: Like so many of the styles popular in the eighteenth century, the federal style relies on classical ideas of proportion as described by Palladio. In this system, each component of an object relates to another in a proscribed manner. The proportions of this stoneware teapot all relate to one another in a precise geometric plan (fig. 51). The upper half of the body is carefully stepped: from the top of the small knob on the cover to the acanthus border, where the handle joins the body, the teapot is a series of gradually widening ovals. The body itself is divided equally into panels emphasized with blue enameled lines. Thus the circular forms of the top are balanced by the rectangular forms of the bottom.

℀ How the Federal Style Became Fashionable

Few events have had a more dramatic impact on the world of style than the discoveries in Italy at Herculaneum in 1738 and at Pompeii in 1748. Both cities had been buried by the violent eruptions of Mount Vesuvius in A.D. 79. Although people had always been fascinated with the civilizations and physical ruins of the classical world (especially during the Renaissance), these new archaeological discoveries marked an opportunity almost unique in history—namely, to study a civilization that had been frozen in time. As the excavations progressed, evidence of the everyday lives of the Romans slowly came into view. Colonnaded houses with fresco-painted walls and mosaic tile floors yielded a wealth of ancient goods, including ceramics, glass, metalwork, and furniture. Roman design could now be studied directly rather than through Renaissance reconstructions and interpretations, and these newly unearthed classical forms had an enormous impact on the world of fashion.

People with the financial means to do so visited the ruins and returned to their homes not only with new ideas about design but also with actual objects from

FIG. 52. Drawing of Pompeian wall decoration. From *Magazin für Freunde des guten Geschmacks* 4, no. 5 (1798): plate 12

FIG. 53. Cabinet handle
on a desk-and-bookcase

antiquity. This beautifully rendered drawing of a Pompeian wall decoration appeared in a German magazine and served as an inspiration for late eighteenth-century interiors (fig. 52).

Those who could not venture to Italy eagerly followed the progress of the excavations through travelers' accounts. This interest in classicism triggered a reevaluation of the Chippendale, or rococo, style, which was then at the height of popularity. The rococo, when compared to the classical, came to be seen as corrupt and overblown based on its close association with the French court; classicism, by contrast, represented a completely new set of values, values that were thought to be embodied in the almost mythical virtues of the ancient world. The predominant design characteristics of the rococo—including rocks, shells, asymmetrical swirls, and fanciful leaves—were replaced by a new set of ornamental elements. Urns, swags, wheat sheaves, and a profusion of geometric forms, especially ovals, reigned supreme. This cabinet handle features a figure in classical garb, perfectly centered in an oval within an oval (fig. 53). The figure may represent the Greek universal mother, Cybele, who is associated with agricultural prosperity and enterprise and was a popular figure in both Roman and Greek mythology.

When it was introduced in America, this new style had an immediate appeal due to its close identification with the much-admired Roman Republic. Although a few objects made in this new style appeared in the colonies prior to the Revolutionary War (Thomas Jefferson owned a writing desk with satinwood banding and an inlaid escutcheon, and Philadelphia silversmith Richard Humphreys crafted a silver urn in 1774 that is not only classical in form but also includes decorative acanthus leaves, rosettes, and beading), the full flowering of the early classical revival in America occurred after the war. The popularity was fueled by the availability of English and French pattern books, the importation of European objects by merchants and returning diplomats, and an influx of European immigrants (both patrons and craftsmen) who widely disseminated knowledge of classicism, bringing it to the attention of an audience eager and able to acquire objects in this latest style.

✸ *Living with Objects in the Federal Style*

In the decades immediately following the Revolution, many Americans amassed great fortunes from land speculation, from the newly opened direct trade routes with the East, and from a greatly increased demand for consumer goods. A wealthy merchant elite emerged, with money to spare and to spend. In addition to investing heavily in stylish household furnishings, these newly rich Americans built lavish dwellings to house their recent purchases or, at the very least, expanded their existing homes to include dining rooms, double parlors, and additional bedrooms. A proliferation of household furnishings designed for specific purposes occurred in the federal era. Consumers acquired new furnishings for their parlors as well, including sofas and card tables. In 1794 a wealthy Connecticut merchant, Oliver Phelps, hired Asher Benjamin, an architect and carpenter, to design and build an addition to his existing house. The addition featured such classical elements as pilasters on either side of the fireplace mantel and design motifs in the plaster decoration also on the fireplace mantel, including swags, cupids, an urn, and a pastoral scene. The room furnishings, as seen in the view of the Phelp's Federal Parlor at Winterthur (fig. 54), also reflect the classical: urn-backed chairs, an inlaid card table, French wallpaper featuring delicate arabesques and cupid-like figures, and to the left of the fireplace, a ladies' sewing table. The upholstered, low easy chair is called a lolling chair, a seating form introduced during this period.

Of all the changes taking place in American homes, perhaps none was more dramatic than the addition of dining rooms. Prior to the Revolution, formal dining in America occurred in various rooms, most often in parlors, bedchambers, or halls. After the war, Americans adopted the then-prevalent English custom of reserving a room specifically for dining. In the case of Mount Vernon, Washington further

FIG. 54. Federal Parlor, Winterthur Museum

refined this trend by adding a *banqueting hall*, a term indicative of the large scale
and frequency of the entertaining he expected to undertake. Furnishing a dining
room required substantial investments—not only in dining tables and sideboards
but also in the accessories needed for fine dining. At an 1805 auction of the con-
tents of the house of William Bingham, one of Philadelphia's wealthiest citizens,
articles for sale were listed room by room. Included for the dining room were looking glasses, chandeliers, knife boxes, sideboards, wine coolers, chairs, many sets of
china, glassware of all sorts, platters, trays, silverware, and plateaus (large elaborate centerpieces for the dining table).

High-style federal interiors differed markedly from interiors of the earlier eighteenth century. Multipurpose rooms were replaced by a profusion of new spaces
dedicated solely to eating, entertaining, and sleeping. Mirrors became increasingly
available, thanks to improvements in glass production, and a preference for the

smooth, unadorned surfaces of veneered furniture and silver services contributed to a highly reflective and bright atmosphere. Thus, federal rooms reflected the optimism and intense nationalism of the time, presenting a much-embellished version of the classical past.

❧ Looking Ahead

The popularity of the early classical revival, or federal, style lasted for a relatively brief period of time in the United States. By 1815 another war with Britain and the beginning of westward expansion contributed to a mind-set that was distinctly different from that which had existed after the Revolution. The light, delicate look of the federal style, which had been appealing only twenty years before, now seemed almost excessive and too reliant on British prototypes. Americans began turning, instead, to a stricter adherence to more archaeologically correct classical forms and embraced a style we know today as empire. This style drew on French prototypes, particularly the work of Napoleon's court designers. Thus, the always-present need for a new or different mode of expression, combined with a changing national image, resulted in the acceptance of this later manifestation of classicism in America.

The federal style did not fade away for long, however. By the late nineteenth century, many cabinetmakers were reproducing federal-style objects. A particularly popular subject for reproduction was the furniture of Duncan Phyfe, a federal cabinetmaker in New York City. With the growing popularity of the colonial revival movement in the early twentieth century, many collectors and museums eager for early classical revival objects drove up prices. Today, federal-style reproductions are readily available in home furnishing stores and catalogues. The size, graceful proportions, and delicate ornamentation of these items fit as easily into modern interiors as they did into the parlors, dining rooms, and morning rooms of the late eighteenth and early nineteenth centuries.

CHAPTER

The Empire Style

FASHIONABLE BETWEEN 1815 AND 1840

Learning to Look

The empire, or later classical revival, style became popular in the United States following the War of 1812 and remained in vogue over the next thirty years, when various revival styles, including rococo, Gothic, and Egyptian, supplanted the classical revival in popular taste. The empire style is named after Napoleon Bonaparte's French empire (1804–14). During his military campaigns to Italy and Egypt at the turn of the nineteenth century, Napoleon visited classical ruins accompanied by a retinue of scholars and artists who, on their return to France, created interiors inspired by the antiquities of classical civilizations. Like the previous federal style, the empire style also drew its inspiration from the classical world but concentrated on design sources from Greece rather than Roman prototypes. However, the differences among the forms and ornament inspired by Greek versus Roman design sources are sometimes difficult to define. Craftsmen in the United States, in particular, interpreted the styles quite freely, and the objects they designed do not clearly reference any one civilization. The empire style is most easily identifiable by its ornamentation, with overt references to Greek design; massive volume; geometric emphasis on line; vibrant colors; and bold textures.

ORNAMENTATION: Both manifestations of the classical revival style, that is, federal and empire, feature abundant references to the ancient world in their choice of decorative motifs. Natural forms such as acanthus leaves, fruit, and flowers abound. What distinguishes the later classical revival style is the preference for animal-form ornamentation, including paws, torsos, and heads. The use of a lion's head as a decorative element, especially as a drawer pull, was widespread in this time period (fig. 55). The highly ornamental treatment of the lion, with its deeply lobed mane, is typical of empire design.

The animal paw feet on this sideboard are another good example of the incorporation of animal motifs on objects (fig. 56). Note also the acanthus leaf carvings over the paws and the ebonized Ionic capitals of the four columns; both were popular design elements when the empire style was fashionable. The mirror is flanked by deeply carved cornucopia spilling forth a bounty of plenty, including grapes and other fruits and elaborate leaves. The use of inlays that was so prevalent in the fed-

FIG. 55. Cabinet handle on a desk-and-bookcase

Fig. 56. Sideboard

eral period gives way in the empire style to elaborate carving, richly veined veneers, and decorative embellishments such as gilt stencils and pressed-glass drawer knobs.

VOLUME: The sideboard also serves as an excellent example of the way in which an empire-style object occupies space. Look back to the federal sideboard (see fig. 46), and the difference in volume between the two objects immediately becomes apparent. This empire sideboard, made in Pittsburgh around 1839, solidly fills the space created by its outline, whereas the tall, slender legs of the New York federal-style sideboard convey a feeling of lightness. The empire-style sideboard, described in the 1828 *Philadelphia Cabinet and Chairmakers' Union Book of Prices for*

Manufacturing Cabinet Wares as a "pedestal end sideboard with open centre," is beautifully proportioned. Note the way in which the crisply carved and intricately pierced cornucopia motif and the highly figured, vertically grained mahogany veneers give the sideboard the appearance of height and increase the perception of the object's imposing size. In addition the substantial, carved feet and the simply framed mirror contribute to the architectural appearance of the object and increase its resemblance to a small building.

LINE: Compared to the attenuated proportions of the federal painted chair (see fig. 47), this empire-style chair presents a much bolder appearance (fig. 57). The chair form, often referred to as a klismos, has close ties to the ancient Greek klismos chair found on gravemarkers and in ancient theaters. Note the wide back, called a tablet, and the outward-curved legs. The degree of curve in its back legs as well as

FIG. 57. Side chair

Fig. 58. Quilt

the depth of the broad crest rail and the trapezoidal seat all illustrate the character-istic line of the empire style. The use of brass inlay for a visually striking decorative effect and the brass stringing that emphasizes the severe rectangularity of the chair also identify this object as later classical revival.

Color: Color assumed increasing importance in the empire period. By 1830 the home was a virtual easel for colors—on furniture, ceramics, and textiles. This quilt, in the sunburst pattern, is made of brightly colored, roller-printed cotton fabrics (fig. 58). The vibrant and contrasting colors, as well as the intricacy of the pattern, create a sense of excitement. As seen on the sideboard and chair, color variety was also achieved through the use of gleaming mahogany veneers, highly polished brass inlays, and contrasting furniture hardware. The use of luster ornament created in metallic oxides gives this teapot (fig. 59) the same gleam that the use of gilt achieved on furniture.

TEXTURE: In this silver tea and coffee service (fig. 60), made in Philadelphia by the silversmithing firm of Chaudron and Rasch, the extensive use of a wide variety of decorative elements gives the pieces a rich, sculpted look, very different from the smooth appearance of the federal silver service made by Joseph Richardson Jr. (see fig. 50). The pieces feature decoration typical of the empire style: each leg of the sugar bowl is topped with a cast goat's head and ends in a cloven hoof; animal heads appear as spouts on the coffee- and teapots; and heavy floral swags encircle the three lids. The rims of all pieces in the set are formed by a decorative band in a guilloche pattern, which looks like two interlaced ribbons. A Greek key design decorates the band encircling the pomegranate finial on the sugar bowl, and a geometric leaf border encircles the base of each piece. Instead of moving easily over the surface of the silver, the eye moves in and out and up and down over the various decorations, almost like a car on a bumpy road.

FIG. 59. Lusterware teapot

FIG. 60. Tea and coffee service

❧ How the Empire Style Became Fashionable

The civilizations that flourished around the Mediterranean Sea from 700 B.C. to
A.D. 400 were the inspiration for the classical revival style both in its more delicate,
decorative phase—known as the federal style—and in its heavier, more archaeologically correct form—referred to as the empire style. Following expeditions to this
area, knowledge of ancient designs spread throughout Europe in the eighteenth
century. Knowledge of Greek and Egyptian designs, in particular, increased after
Napoleon and his entourage returned to France and publicized their findings.
Charles Percier and Pierre Fontaine, designers who had traveled to Egypt with

Napoleon, set the standard for fashionable interiors with the publication of their drawings based on prototypes from ancient civilizations (fig. 61).

Wealthy Americans traveled to see ancient sites and returned to their homes fired with enthusiasm for the ancient world and with a desire to furnish their homes in the latest style. Even if they did not travel abroad, Americans of both great and middling wealth could learn of the new style from design books and periodicals that contained images of Roman, Greek, and Egyptian antiquities, such as *Household Furniture and Interior Decoration*, printed in 1807. Thomas Hope, an English collector and patron of the arts, published the book to showcase his own home and furnishings in London. Rudolph Ackermann published the periodical *Repository of the Arts* in London between 1809 and 1828 to promote the latest designs. Architect Benjamin Henry Latrobe, who was professionally trained and well known in America for the buildings he designed, also laid out domestic interiors and designed furniture in the empire style. His most famous commission was for Dolley and

FIG. 61. Interior design. From Charles Percier and Pierre Fontaine, *Choix des plus célèbres maisons de plaisance* (Paris, 1809), plate 31

Fig. 62. Empire Parlor, Winterthur Museum

James Madison's Oval Room in the White House. In addition, Americans who traveled to England, France, and Italy as well as Greece and even Egypt could ship European objects back to their homes in America or, upon returning, patronize well-known local craftspeople, many of whom had emigrated from Europe.

❧ Living with Objects in the Empire Style

The Empire Parlor at Winterthur displays many of the forms a relatively wealthy family might have owned in this time period: a center table, klismos chairs, twin pier tables, an upright grand piano on the far wall, and wall brackets supporting two urns made of the highly desirable French porcelain (fig. 62). The center table was a relatively new furniture form in this time period; family and guests would gather around it in the evening to read, play games, and conduct polite conversations. As in the earlier federal era, room furnishings continued to reflect the intense patriotism of the time. Note the eagle motif on the looking glass above the fireplace as well as on the wall brackets. The French porcelain urns feature portraits of Washington and Lafayette.

Not only the elite chose to furnish their homes in the empire style, however. Printed periodicals and advertisements disseminated designs to many levels of society, and industrial and technological developments increased the variety and availability of household goods. As seen in this silhouette collage, made in 1842 by Auguste Edouart, a prosperous, middle-class family relaxes in their parlor, complete with klismos chairs, a scroll-armed sofa, a round table, and swagged draperies at the window (fig. 63). Whereas a prosperous young couple furnishing their first home in the 1730s probably patronized a local craftsman and ordered custom-made furniture, in the 1830s a similar couple likely had other options. They might visit

Fig. 63. Silhouette

an auction house or warehouse in Boston, Philadelphia, or an outlying town or county seat to compare and choose finished pieces offered by furnituremakers who had banded together to sell their wares more efficiently and profitably.

✎ *Looking Ahead*

The empire style, fashionable in the United States from about 1815 until 1840, more visibly reflects a deepening interest in the classical inspirations that were evident in federal-style objects. Published images of ancient ruins and greater opportunities for travel in the relative peace that followed the Napoleonic Wars influenced not only the designers and makers of household goods but also the consumers, who were drawn to careful imitations of the archaeological remains of antiquity. While design features from all classical civilizations found favor, the simple, dignified forms derived from Greek precedents were especially popular, as demonstrated by the many Greek revival buildings (mimicking the ancient temple form) that were constructed at this time. Furniture decorated with classical motifs (or designed to replicate the furniture that was depicted on ancient vases or wall paintings) as well as glassware, ceramics, and textiles with classical images were available for purchase throughout the United States. The empire style developed at a particularly favorable time in the expanding country, when wealthy consumers' desires for objects like those they saw in cosmopolitan European design sources could be met, thanks to modern manufacturing and transportation systems. However, even as the empire style began to find favor with the growing middle class, wealthier patrons of the decorative arts had moved on to the newer trend, namely the various revival styles that were to dominate fashion for the remainder of the nineteenth century.

Pugin's Gothic furniture.

Published by R. Ackermann, 96 Strand.

CHAPTER 7

Rococo Revival & Gothic Revival Styles

FASHIONABLE BETWEEN 1830 AND 1860

Learning to Look

*S*everal revival styles based on historical precedents became fashionable in the mid nineteenth century. Interest in Greek and Egyptian styles continued at the same time that interest in Renaissance, Elizabethan, rococo, and Gothic revival decorative arts objects developed. Sometimes these styles are grouped together as *Victorian* (for England's Queen Victoria, who reigned from 1837 until her death in 1901). Two styles in particular, rococo revival and Gothic revival, were fashionable in the years before the Civil War. Designers working in these styles looked to a romanticized past, drawing inspiration from a fascination with nature or from the mysterious and remote Middle Ages (fig. 64). Objects in the rococo revival and Gothic revival styles can be most easily identified by their lavish ornament and their commanding volume, or mass.

ORNAMENTATION: The rococo style features exotic and naturalistic motifs in which the curved line predominates. Like rococo-style objects from a century earlier, rococo revival–style objects also incorporate naturalistic ornament and curved lines but in

FIG. 64. Gothic-style interior design. From Augustus Charles Pugin, *Gothic Furniture* (London, 1828), frontispiece

a heavier, more robust, more three-dimensional way. In this center table, for example, the interconnected C scrolls and S scrolls of the legs and the flowers, fruits,
scrolls, and cascades on the tabletop all reflect the rococo taste for realistic natural
forms (fig. 65). However, here in the revival style, the abundant carving and naturalistic motifs dominate the form rather than being integrated into it. To compare
the eighteenth-century rococo with its revival counterpart, refer to figure 37, the
Philadelphia high chest. Note the striking differences in visual effect between the
two objects: in the high chest, the ornamentation complements the object's form
whereas in the revival-style center table, the ornamentation *becomes* the object. The
same use of asymmetrical exuberant ornament can be seen in this brass furniture

FIG. 65. Center table

Fig. 66. Brass
pendant ring handle

pull, where a naturalistic leaf form curls around and embraces the bail (or pull) much as a growing vine climbs a post (fig. 66).

Gothic revival ornamentation is equally obvious but much more restrained than its rococo revival counterpart. Gothic revival designers also looked to earlier times for inspiration, namely to the Gothic buildings throughout Europe that date from 1100 to the early 1500s. This design for a Gothic revival room taken from the design books of Augustus Charles Pugin shows the fashionable homeowner how to create a Gothic interior overflowing with references to the Middle Ages (see fig. 64). The architecture of the room imitates cathedral architecture with its use of pointed arches within the doorway that frames the room and in the bookcase to the right of the fireplace. Within the room, the Gothic revival–style furniture continues the richly ornamental approach to design, displaying pointed arches, fretwork, and tracery.

VOLUME: Objects in these two revival styles occupy space in a compelling manner. This Gothic revival–style chair would have dominated any room in which it was

Fig. 67. Chair

placed through the exaggerated height of the back, which gives it a very architectural appearance, suggesting a cathedral (fig. 67). Notice also the decorative vocabulary of a cathedral, including the Gothic pointed arch, the interlacing tracery on the chair back with trefoil and quatrefoil openings, and the crockets (the small, protruding, hooklike elements that imitate furled leaves).

The heavy, bulbous shape of this rococo revival–style teapot (fig. 68) with its bulging rectangular-shape body and high-domed lid with flaring knob sets it apart from teapots made in earlier styles. In addition, this teapot features substantially more decoration, not only in embellishments to the basic form but also on the body of the pot. The transfer-printed design completely fills all available space: the stipple-ground borders are composed of leafy cartouches and sprigs, and the landscape includes buildings and water and foliage forms.

❧ How the Rococo Revival & Gothic Revival Styles Became Fashionable

As with earlier styles, objects in the rococo revival or Gothic revival styles gained favor through their publication in design books and through their visibility as the

FIG. 68. Teapot

belongings of wealthy, powerful people. Influential books by Englishmen Augustus Charles Pugin and his son, A.W. N. Pugin, provided accurate drawings of design elements from Gothic furniture and architecture of the 1400s. Alexander Jackson Davis and his friend Andrew Jackson Downing also published designs for Gothic revival interiors. By the mid nineteenth century, printed sources that contained images of these room settings became more widely available to potential customers than they had been in the eighteenth century. Subscription magazines proliferated. Periodicals such as *Godey's Magazine and Lady's Book* carried images of new interior designs and instructions on how to achieve them into countless American homes (fig. 69). *Godey's*, the first and most widely read American journal for women, was published in Philadelphia from 1830 to 1890 and featured line engravings of "cottage furniture" as well as designs for curtains. This 1854 image of a curtain design is described as "the entire front of a drawing room . . . which would do no discredit to the days of the monarch for whom it is called, Louis XIV."

Great international expositions, or fairs, also helped disseminate information on the newest fashions in household furnishings. Starting about midcentury, pride

FIG. 69. "Fashion Plates for Decorating Parlor Windows," *Godey's Magazine and Lady's Book* 49 (July 1854)

in the products of increasingly industrialized manufacturing systems merged with nationalism, motivating representatives from many countries to participate in great fairs. These included the Great Exhibition of 1851 in London, the Exhibition of the Industry of All Nations in New York in 1853–54, and the Exposition Universelle in Paris in 1855. Such grand fairs touted manufacturing and artistic achievements, and designers and artists received public acclaim in the press and through the patronage of influential trendsetters.

The middle years of the nineteenth century were also a time of great technological advances that significantly affected the decoration of American homes. Increased factory production permitted manufacturers to produce large quantities of finished goods in various price ranges. The selling of household goods occurred on a larger scale as well. In the furniture trades, for example, customers (especially those in large cities) could shop in warerooms and select from many more pieces of finished furniture than had been available in earlier years. In Baltimore in 1800, a furniture seller had fewer than 40 finished pieces in his inventory. Twenty-six years later, another maker offered 160 finished pieces. In 1855 yet another maker had 900 pieces.

The increased scale of production and distribution offered more choices to more people. In the eighteenth century only the wealthiest people could afford to have a portrait painted of family members. By the mid nineteenth century, new photographic processes put family portraits within the reach of many. In the 1850s, members of the du Pont family in Wilmington, Delaware, had a carte de visite (a photograph on paper rather than tin or glass) made of their children (fig. 70). Note the plaid dresses worn by the young girls. Much as the revival of the rococo and Gothic styles in decorative furnishings reflect a widespread interest in a romanticized past, so does the use of plaid or tartan in costume. It harks back to the last Scottish pretender to the English throne (Bonny Prince Charlie) and his unsuccessful attempts to regain the English throne. Plaid also became linked to Queen Victoria and her family's beloved summer home in Scotland—Balmoral. While summering there, the royal family adopted highland dress, resulting in the popularization of plaid dresses, scarves, kilts, and trousers—a popularity that has never totally faded from the fashion scene. Note also the Gothic revival–style chair in the photograph. It is essentially a simpler version of the much more elaborate (and more expensive) chair seen in figure 67.

⸎ *Living with Objects in the Rococo Revival & Gothic Revival Styles*

Although the rococo revival style evoked the eighteenth-century French royal court and the Gothic revival style recalled medieval churches, objects produced in these styles were made to suit the lives of nineteenth-century Americans. Thus, revival-style objects embodied the aesthetic of a past time, but they did not imitate the actual artifacts of those earlier centuries.

An architect building a home with a Gothic revival exterior was not bound by medieval convention for its interior plan. Such a house would have contained whatever room arrangements and furnishings the modern inhabitant found practical. Rococo revival furnishings were more often found in the parlor and in bedchambers than in the dining room. In the dining room, one might find the style reflected in media such as ceramics, glass, and silver. This ewer, made by Samuel Kirk of Baltimore, probably held a place of honor on a sideboard (fig. 71). The elaborateness of the form, which is covered almost entirely with repoussé ornament (decoration

Opposite:
FIG. 70. Du Pont family carte de visite
FIG. 71. Ewer

produced with hammers and punches, creating a raised design inside the vessel), would have sent a clear message to visitors that the owners were not only wealthy but well-versed in the latest stylistic trends.

Although rococo revival–style dining room furnishings might have been rare, center tables for parlors, popular forms during the heyday of the empire style, often exhibited rococo revival characteristics. Improved lighting technology helped make these tables the center of family life or, in very formal parlors, the focal point for visitors. Solar lamps were one of several types of lighting that greatly improved visibility during evening hours (fig. 72). With its curling leaves and waterfall-like cascades, this solar lamp would have been an appropriate fixture for an elaborate rococo revival center table such as that in figure 65.

A rococo revival furniture suite might include a sofa, several chairs, and a center table, where the family could gather during leisure hours (fig. 73). A parlor com-

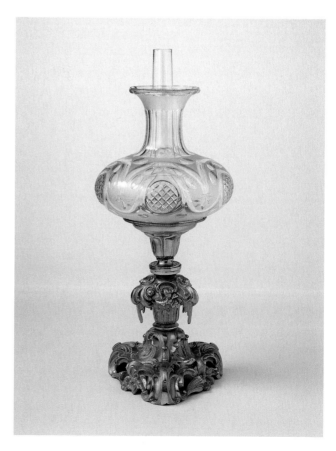

FIG. 72. Solar lamp

Opposite:
FIG. 73. Rococo Revival
Parlor, Winterthur Museum
(no longer on view)

plete with a center table, a matching suite of furniture, an oversize mirror, and an elaborate chandelier signaled the status of the family to anyone who visited the home. Displaying landscape views on the parlor wall also indicated awareness of the world outside the confines of the home.

The Gothic revival style (as seen in fig. 64), with its connotations of medieval, ecclesiastical values of spirituality and learning, was considered most appropriate for halls, libraries, and dining rooms. Although the Gothic revival style was applied more often to architecture than the rococo revival style, it was a less popular option for interior furnishings. Surviving Gothic revival furniture is less common and less well-documented than was rococo revival furniture. Nevertheless, Gothic motifs appear on a wide variety of objects, from printed textiles to cast-iron parlor stoves, silver pitchers, and pressed-glass windowpanes. An appliquéd patchwork quilt from the 1850s includes a piece of fabric with a medieval bishop framed in a Gothic arch (fig. 74). The fabric may well have been purchased with the specific intent of cutting it up into pieces for inclusion in a patchwork quilt such as this one. This would have signaled that the middle-class housewife who most likely made the quilt was conversant with the latest fashion. Notice also how the quilter has mixed both Gothic imagery (the bishop) and rococo revival decorative motifs in the textile through the use of floral motifs, a popular form in the latter style.

❧ Looking Ahead

By the middle of the nineteenth century, Americans were confronted by the great social, economic, and political upheavals that came with progress that resulted from rapid population growth, industrialization, and the onset of the Civil War. Yet, in their homes, they recalled and reflected on the past by selecting furnishings designed in several historical revival styles. Makers of these furnishings drew inspiration from the supposed simplicity of the Middle Ages, from the eighteenth-century French court, from the Renaissance, and from cultures they perceived as exotic (for example, Japanese, Indian, and Turkish). Faced with a proliferation of various influences as the turn of the century approached, people chose objects in styles that were both practical and symbolic. Their choices demonstrate how they used space in their homes, how they thought about history and about the modernization of their own time, how they defined men's and women's roles, and how they perceived people from other countries and other cultures.

Fig. 74. Bedspread

Perceptions of the "appropriateness" of various styles changed over time, and consumers began to reject prolific and varied ornamentation. In the decorative arts, as in politics and economics, leaders spoke out against the decadence of excessively ornamented furnishings and championed the rights of wage earners who were forced to perform the specialized, repetitive tasks required by industrialized manufacturing. From the 1880s to the early 1900s, developers of new styles, specifically the arts and crafts style, called for simple, "honest" production methods. These same values were the impetus behind another revival style—the colonial revival—which was encouraged by the celebration of the one hundredth anniversary of the Declaration of Independence. Late nineteenth-century Americans who embraced this new style turned again to America's past, reviving some of the styles that had been fashionable in the colonies and young republic, in particular Queen Anne, Chippendale, and federal. The enthusiasm for the revival styles, in particular Gothic and rococo, has not enjoyed a re-revival in the late twentieth century. Rather, consumers prefer the styles of the colonial and early national period to their revival counterparts.

CONCLUSION

Henry Francis du Pont, Winterthur & Styles

$\mathcal{L}$ike many Americans, Henry Francis du Pont was touched by a fascination with objects from his country's past, and in 1920 he began collecting American "antiques" with great enthusiasm. In the room settings he created at Winterthur, he exploited various styles, using the repeated design characteristics of each to achieve graceful visual harmonies. His goal was to assemble a comprehensive collection that would document the lives of early Americans and showcase the exceptional skills of American craftsmen. He realized that goal. The Winterthur collection offers visitors the opportunity not only to think about people in the past and the stylistic choices they made but also to consider the choices we make today. In short, it offers us the opportunity to more fully understand the concept of style.

There are, of course, many styles not covered in this book. The styles of the late nineteenth and twentieth centuries are not explored, nor are the many ethnic or regional variations such as Pennsylvania German, Shaker, or vernacular traditions. In part, the decision to limit the discussion to the 1640–1860 time frame was based on the strengths of Winterthur's collection. In a letter to a friend later in his life, du Pont wrote that he had deliberately decided not to expand his collecting into the twentieth century because he felt it would dilute his focus and that he preferred to concentrate on a shorter time frame in order to explore it in depth. In addition, many of the ethnic and regional variations are based on the major style periods explored in this book. Studying them closely lays a solid foundation for learning more about other areas of style.

Developing the ability to recognize style, any style, must begin with the habit of active looking—paying careful attention to comparisons and contrasts. In addition, recognizing style involves learning something of the culture in which the style was produced, to better understand the people who designed, made, sold, and purchased the objects we love to collect today.

For information on styles not addressed here, please consult *Suggested Readings* at the back of the book.

RESOURCES

STYLE CHARACTERISTICS FROM THE SEVENTEENTH CENTURY TO EMPIRE:

Style	SEVENTEENTH CENTURY	WILLIAM AND MARY
Dates	1620–80	1680–1720
Description	Abundance of ornamentation, predominant straight lines, and a liberal use of vibrant color.	Emphasis on vertical line and a unity of structure, with lavish decorative ornamentation based on curved lines, robust textures, and contrasting colors.
Chairs		
Case furniture		
Silver		
Drawer and cabinet handles		

AN ILLUSTRATED TIME LINE

QUEEN ANNE

1720–55

Emphasis on the curved line, which becomes the outline of the object; a strict adherence to classical proportions and the restrained use of ornamentation and color.

CHIPPENDALE

1755–90

Lavish ornamentation, the use of vertical lines to outline furniture forms, asymmetrical ornamentation, and contrasting textures.

FEDERAL

1790–1815

Delicate scale, straight lines, vibrant colors, smooth textures, classical proportions, and classical ornamentation.

EMPIRE

1815–40

Ornamentation with overt references to Greek design, massive volume, geometric emphasis on line, vibrant colors, and bold textures.

SUGGESTED READINGS

GENERAL REFERENCE

Bates, Elizabeth Bidwell, and Jonathan L. Fairbanks. *American Furniture: 1620 to the Present*. New York: Richard Marek Publishers, 1981.

Fitzgerald, Oscar P. *Four Centuries of American Furniture*. Radnor, Pa.: Wallace-Homestead Book Co., 1995.

Palmer, Arlene. *Glass in Early America: Selections from the Henry Francis du Pont Winterthur Museum*. Winterthur, Del.: Henry Francis du Pont Winterthur Museum, 1993.

Quimby, Ian M. G. *American Silver at Winterthur*. Winterthur, Del.: Henry Francis du Pont Winterthur Museum, 1995.

Richards, Nancy E., and Nancy Goyne Evans. *New England Furniture at Winterthur: Queen Anne and Chippendale Periods*. Winterthur, Del.: Henry Francis du Pont Winterthur Museum, 1997.

Thornton, Peter. *Authentic Decor: The Domestic Interior, 1620–1920*. New York: Viking Press, 1984.

Weidman, Gregory P. *Furniture in Maryland, 1740–1940*. Baltimore: Maryland Historical Society, 1984.

SEVENTEENTH CENTURY

Fairbanks, Jonathan, and Robert F. Trent. *New England Begins: The Seventeenth Century*. Boston: Museum of Fine Arts, 1982.

Thornton, Peter. *Seventeenth-Century Interior Decoration in England, France, and Holland*. New Haven: Yale University Press for the Paul Mellon Centre for Studies in British Art, 1978.

WILLIAM AND MARY

Baarsen, Renier, et al. *Courts and Colonies: The William and Mary Style in Holland, England, and America.* Washington, D.C.: Smithsonian Institution Press, 1988.

Forman, Benno M. *American Seating Furniture, 1630–1730: An Interpretive Catalogue.* New York: W. W. Norton, 1988.

Trent, Robert F. "The Early Baroque in Early America: The William and Mary Style." In *American Furniture with Related Decorative Arts, 1660–1830*, edited by Gerald W. R. Ward. New York: Hudson Hills Press, 1992.

QUEEN ANNE

Jobe, Brock W. "The Late Baroque in Colonial America: The Queen Anne Style." In *American Furniture with Related Decorative Arts, 1660–1830*, edited by Gerald W. R. Ward. New York: Hudson Hills Press, 1992.

Zimmerman, Philip D. "Regionalism in American Furniture Studies." *In Perspectives in American Furniture*, edited by Gerald W. R. Ward. New York: W. W. Norton, 1988.

CHIPPENDALE

Bushman, Richard L. *The Refinement of America: Persons, Houses, Cities.* New York: Alfred A. Knopf, 1992.

Heckscher, Morrison H., and Leslie Greene Bowman. *American Rococo, 1750–1775: Elegance in Ornament.* New York: Metropolitan Museum of Art, Los Angeles County Museum of Art, 1992.

Hummel, Charles F. *With Hammer in Hand: The Dominy Craftsmen of East Hampton, New York.* Charlottesville: University Press of Virginia for the Henry Francis du Pont Winterthur Museum, 1968.

Jobe, Brock, and Myrna Kaye. *New England Furniture: The Colonial Era: Selections from the Society for the Preservation of New England Antiquities.* Boston: Houghton Mifflin Co., 1984.

FEDERAL

Garvan, Beatrice. *Federal Philadelphia: The Athens of the Western World*. Philadelphia: Philadelphia Museum of Art, 1987.

Michie, Thomas. "Neoclassicism in the New Nation: The Federal Style." In *American Furniture with Related Decorative Arts, 1660–1830*, edited by Gerald W. R. Ward. New York: Hudson Hills Press, 1992.

Montgomery, Charles F. *American Furniture: The Federal Period, 1788–1825*. New York: Viking Press, 1966.

EMPIRE

Cooper, Wendy A. *Classical Taste in America, 1800–1840*. New York: Abbeville Press, 1993.

Fennimore, Donald L. "Egyptian Influence in Early Nineteenth-Century American Furniture." *Antiques* 137, no. 5 (May 1990): 1190–1201.

Talbott, Page. *Classical Savannah: Fine and Decorative Arts, 1800–1840*. Savannah, Ga.: Telfair Museum of Art, 1995.

Weidman, Gregory R., et al. *Classical Maryland, 1815–1845: Fine and Decorative Arts from the Golden Age*. Baltimore: Maryland Historical Society, 1993.

ROCOCO REVIVAL & GOTHIC REVIVAL

Ames, Kenneth L. *Death in the Dining Room and Other Tales of Victorian Culture*. Philadelphia: Temple University Press, 1992.

Douglas, Ed Polk. "Rococo Revival: John Henry Belter." In *Nineteenth-Century Furniture: Innovation, Revival, and Reform*. Introduction by Mary Jean Madigan. New York: Billboard Publication, 1982.

Hindle, Brooke, and Steven Lubar. *Engines of Changes: The American Industrial Revolution, 1790–1860*. Washington, D.C.: Smithsonian Institution Press, 1986.

Howe, Katherine S., and David B. Warren. *The Gothic Revival Style in America, 1830–1870*. Houston: Museum of Fine Arts, 1976.

Nineteenth-Century America: Furniture and Other Decorative Arts. Introduction by Berry B. Tracy. New York: Metropolitan Museum of Art, 1970.

LIST OF ILLUSTRATIONS

INTRODUCTION: *Understanding Style*

Fɪɢ. 1.
Lady's cabinet and writing table
Baltimore, 1795–1810
Mahogany, satinwood, red cedar
H. 62 ⅛", W. 30 ⅞", D. 22 ¼"
57.68 Museum purchase

Fɪɢ. 2.
Chest
Massachusetts, 1678
Red oak, poplar, maple, walnut
H. 42", W. 44 ¾", D. 19 ⅞"
57.541 Gift of Henry Francis du Pont

Fɪɢ. 3.
Side chair
New York City, 1765–80
Mahogany
H. 38 ½", W. 23 ½", D. 21 ¾"
58.1784.1 Bequest of Henry Francis du Pont

Fɪɢ. 4.
Salver
Bancroft Woodcock, Wilmington, Del., 1754–75
Silver
H. 1 ⁹⁄₁₆", Diam. 8 ¹⁵⁄₁₆"
51.63 Gift of Henry Francis du Pont

Fɪɢ. 5.
Desk-and-bookcase
Baltimore, 1790–1800
Mahogany, ebony, satinwood, zebrawood, tulip,
pine, hard oak
H. 102 ⅝", W. 42 ¼", D. 22 ⅝"
57.775 Bequest of Henry Francis du Pont

Fɪɢ. 6.
Plate
Pennsylvania, 1793
Lead-glazed earthenware
H. 1 ¼", Diam. 15 ¹⁄₁₆"
67.1670 Bequest of Henry Francis du Pont

Fɪɢ. 7.
Side chair
Boston, 1700–1720
Beech, oak, maple
H. 43 ¼", W. 18", D. 18 ½"
81.46 Gift of Henry Francis du Pont

Fɪɢ. 8.
Side chair
Attributed to John Leech, Boston, 1735–60
Black walnut
H. 40 ¼", W. 22", D. 20 ⅛"
54.523 Gift of Henry Francis du Pont

CHAPTER 1: *The Seventeenth-Century Style*

Fig. 9.
DESIGN
From G. Charmeton, *Diverses ornemens pour servir à toutes sortes d'artisans* (Paris, 165?)
NK1115 S43 F, Winterthur Library

Fig. 10.
JOINED CHEST
Attributed to Thomas Dennis, Ipswich, Mass., dated 1676
Red oak, white oak
H. 31 $^{11}/_{16}$", W. 49 $^5/_8$", D. 22 $^5/_8$"
82.276 Funds for acquisitions supplied by The Honorable Walter H. Annenberg, Mr. and Mrs. George P. Bissell Jr., J. Bruce Bredin, Mrs. Donald F. Carpenter, Mrs. Lammot du Pont Copeland, Mrs. Henry Belin du Pont, John T. Dorrance Jr., Mr. and Mrs. Edward B. du Pont and Mrs. M. Lewis du Pont, Mrs. Reynolds du Pont, William K. du Pont, Mrs. George B. Foote Jr., Charles J. Harrington, Mr. and Mrs. George S. Harrington, Willis F. Harrington, Mr. and Mrs. Rodney M. Layton, Henry S. McNeil, Mrs. G. Burton Pearson Jr., Stephen A. Trentman, Mrs. Neal S. Wood

Fig. 11.
DRAWER HANDLE
United States, 1700
Brass
H. 1 $^3/_4$", W. 1 $^3/_4$", D. $^2/_3$"
58.102.20 Museum purchase with funds pr vided by Henry Francis du Pont

Fig. 12.
ARMCHAIR
New England, 1660–1700
Oak, ash, hickory
H. 41 $^1/_4$", W. 23 $^3/_4$", D. 19 $^3/_4$"
58.681 Gift of Henry Francis du Pont

Fig. 13.
PORTRAIT OF AN UNKNOWN WOMAN
Attributed to Gerret Duyckinck, New York City, 1690–1710
Oil on panel
H. 31 $^1/_2$", W. 24 $^1/_4$"
56.565 Bequest of Henry Francis du Pont

Fig. 14.
CAUDLE CUP
Robert Sanderson, Boston, 1652–83
Silver
H. 5", W. 7 $^5/_8$"
61.504 Gift of Henry Francis du Pont

Fig. 15.
SACK BOTTLE
England, dated 1645
Tin-glazed earthenware (delftware)
H. 6 $^1/_4$", W. 4 $^3/_8$"
64.681 Bequest of Henry Francis du Pont

Fig. 16
SEVENTEENTH-CENTURY ROOM
Winterthur Museum (no longer on view)

Fig. 17.
QUILT
Portugal, 1675–1725
Silk
W. 87 $^1/_2$", L. 101 $^1/_2$"
54.49 Gift of Henry Francis du Pont

CHAPTER 2: *The William and Mary Style*

Fig. 18.
ARMCHAIR
New England, 1700–1715
Red oak, maple
H. 35 $^1/_3$", W. 24", D. 27 $^1/_2$"
58.553 Gift of Henry Francis du Pont

CHAPTER 3: *The Queen Anne Style*

FIG. 30.
TEAPOT
England, 1730–45
Lead glass
H. 6 $^{3}/_{16}$", W. 8 $^{1}/_{16}$"
81.67 Museum purchase

FIG. 31.
HIGH CHEST
South Windsor, Conn., dated 1736
Maple, pine
H. 61", W. 41 $^{3}/_{8}$", D. 25 $^{5}/_{8}$"
54.507 Gift of Henry Francis du Pont

FIG. 32.
MRS. CHARLES WILLING (ANNE SHIPPEN)
Robert Feke, Philadelphia, 1746
Oil on canvas
H. 50", W. 40"
69.134 Gift of Mr. and Mrs. Alfred E. Bissell in
memory of Henry Francis du Pont

FIG. 33.
BEDCOVER
India, 1690–1760
Cotton
L. 111 $^{1}/_{4}$", W. 87 $^{1}/_{2}$"
60.780 Gift of Miss Gertrude Brinckle

FIG. 34.
CABINET HANDLE ON A DESK-AND-BOOKCASE
John Welch, Boston, 1743–48
Mahogany, white pine, cedar, ash, brass
H. 97 $^{1}/_{4}$", W. 42 $^{7}/_{8}$", D. 23 $^{1}/_{2}$"
60.1134 Gift of Henry Francis du Pont

FIG. 35.
TANKARDS *(left to right)*
William Holmes Sr. or Jr., Boston, 1760–80
Silver
H. 8 $^{1}/_{2}$", W. 7 $^{7}/_{16}$"
80.111 Gift of Mrs. C. Newbold Taylor

Philip Syng Jr., Philadelphia, ca. 1745
Silver
H. 8 $^{1}/_{16}$", W. 7 $^{3}/_{16}$"
61.620 Gift of Henry Francis du Pont

Simeon Soumaine, New York City, 1730–50
Silver
H. 6 $^{3}/_{4}$", W. 5"
63.524 Gift of Henry Francis du Pont

FIG. 36.
CECIL BEDROOM
Winterthur Museum

CHAPTER 4: *The Chippendale Style*

FIG. 37.
HIGH CHEST
Philadelphia, 1765–80
Swietenia, tulip, oak, pine
H. 90 $^{1}/_{4}$", W. 46 $^{5}/_{8}$", D. 25 $^{1}/_{2}$"
58.592 Gift of Henry Francis du Pont

FIG. 38.
SALVER
John Heath, United States, 1765
Silver
H. 1 $^{5}/_{8}$", Diam. 15 $^{1}/_{8}$"
59.2301 Gift of Henry Francis du Pont

FIG. 39.
SIDE CHAIR
Philadelphia, 1760–75
Mahogany, yellow pine, cedar
H. 37 $^{3}/_{4}$", W. 23 $^{1}/_{2}$", D. 22 $^{3}/_{4}$"
52.240.3 Gift of Henry Francis du Pont

FIG. 40.
CABINET HANDLE ON A DESK-AND-BOOKCASE
United States, 1785–95
Mahogany, pine, brass
H. 95 $^{1}/_{2}$", W. 37 $^{1}/_{2}$", D. 20 $^{1}/_{2}$"
56.23 Gift of Henry Francis du Pont

FIG. 41.
TEAPOT
England, 1760–75
Redware
H. 5 ³/₁₆", W. 8 ³/₈"
71.191 Gift of Mr. and Mrs. John Mayer

FIG. 42.
CHAIR DESIGNS
From Thomas Chippendale, *The Gentleman and Cabinet-Maker's Director* (London: By the author, 1754), plate 15.
RBR NK2542 C54, Winterthur Library

FIG. 43.
QUILT
England, 1775–85
Cotton
W. 84 ¼", L. 84 ½"
60.67 Museum purchase

FIG. 44.
BLACKWELL PARLOR
Winterthur Museum

FIG. 45.
MRS. BENJAMIN RUSH (JULIA STOCKTON)
Charles Willson Peale
Philadelphia, 1776
Oil on canvas
H. 49", W. 39 ³/₁₆"
60.382 Gift Mrs. T. Charlton Henry

CHAPTER 5: *The Federal Style*

FIG. 46.
SIDEBOARD
New York City, 1795–1805
Mahogany, white pine, tulip, ash, satinwood
H. 41 ¼", W. 79 ½", D. 28 ⁵/₈"
57.850 Bequest of Henry Francis du Pont

FIG. 47.
SIDE CHAIR
Probably Philadelphia, 1801
Soft maple, white pine, silk
H. 38 ³/₈", W. 21 ¾", D. 21 ¾"
57.21.2 Museum purchase

FIG. 48.
HIS EXCELL\CY GEORGE WASHINGTON, ESQ\R
Published by John Coles, Boston, 1782
Engraving on laid paper
H. 13 ¼", W. 9 ½"
58.2412 Bequest of Henry Francis du Pont

FIG. 49.
BEDSPREAD
Philadelphia, 1780–1800
Cotton
W. 103 ¼", L. 106 ¼"
63.48 Museum purchase

FIG. 50.
TEA AND COFFEE SERVICE
Joseph Richardson Jr., Philadelphia, ca. 1795
Silver
(clockwise, from left)
Sugar urn: H. 10 ½", W. 4 ¹³/₁₆"
Waste bowl: H. 5 ¾", Diam. 6 ½"
Coffeepot: H. 13 ¹/₁₆", W. 12 ⁷/₈"
Teapot: H. 5 ³/₈", W. 10 ¹⁵/₁₆"
Teapot: H. 5 ⁷/₈", W. 11 ⁵/₈"
Creamer: H. 7", W. 5 ³/₁₆"
57.822–.827 Gift of Henry Francis du Pont

FIG. 51.
TEAPOT
Staffordshire, England, 1790–1820
Stoneware
H. 5 ¹⁵/₁₆", W. 4 ¹/₁₆", L. 8 ¹³/₁₆"
91.60 Gift of Mr. and Mrs. James C. Manning in memory of the Keyser family of Germantown, Pennsylvania

FIG. 52.
DRAWING OF POMPEIAN WALL DECORATION
From *Magazin für Freunde des guten Geschmacks*
4, no. 5 (1798): plate 12.

FIG. 53.
CABINET HANDLE ON A DESK-AND-BOOKCASE
Edmund Johnson, Salem, Mass., 1793–1805
Mahogany, white pine, brass
H. 93 ¾", W. 66 ⅝", D. 20"
57.844 Bequest of Henry Francis du Pont

FIG. 54.
FEDERAL PARLOR
Winterthur Museum

CHAPER 6: *The Empire Style*

FIG. 55.
CABINET HANDLE ON A DESK-AND-BOOKCASE
Joseph B. Barry, Philadelphia, 1808–15
Mahogany, brass
H. 50 ⅞", W. 87 ⅝", D. 25 ¾"
88.8.1 Museum purchase

FIG. 56.
SIDEBOARD
Philadelphia, 1837–44
Mahogany, poplar, pine, glass, marble
H. 55 ⅝", W. 67 ½", D. 23 ⅛"
72.296 Museum purchase

FIG. 57.
SIDE CHAIR
Philadelphia, 1810–20
Mahogany, ash, rosewood, brass
H. 31 ¾", W. 18 ⅞", D. 25 ¾"
88.35.2 Museum purchase

FIG. 58.
QUILT
Rebecca Scattergood Savery, Philadelphia, 1827
Cotton
H. 31 ¾", W. 22 ¾"
97.22 Museum purchase with funds provided
by the Estate of Mrs. Samuel Pettit and additional funds by Mr. Samuel Pettit in memory of
his wife

FIG. 59.
TEAPOT
Sunderland, England, 1825–50
Lusterware
H. 5 ¾", W. 8 ¾"
64.1299.7 Bequest of Henry Francis du Pont

FIG. 60.
TEA AND COFFEE SERVICE
Chaudron and Rasch, Philadelphia, 1809–12
Silver
(from left)
Waste bowl: H. 6 ¼", W. 7 ⁵⁄₁₆"
Sugar urn: H. 10 ⅝", W. 6 ³⁄₁₆"
Creamer: H. 7 ⅛", W. 5 ⁹⁄₁₆"
Coffeepot: H. 13", W. 12 ⅝"
Teapot: H. 9 ⅞", W. 11"
75.80.1–.5
Gift of Mr. and Mrs. Henry Pleasants III in
memory of Maria Wilkins Smith, 1975

FIG. 61.
INTERIOR DESIGN
From Charles Percier and Pierre Fontaine,
Choix des plus célèbres maisons de plaisance
(Paris, 1809), plate 31.
RBR 7594 P42c PF, Winterthur Library

FIG. 62.
EMPIRE PARLOR
Winterthur Museum